THIS BOOK BELONGS TO:

PRAISE FOR *SO MUCH TO CELEBRATE*

"Y'all are going to fall in love with Katie Jacobs. She's a modern Southerner who knows how to throw a stylish party with grace, charm, and really good food. Best of all, she reminds us that celebrating has one aim—to bring those you love together."

—ELIZABETH MAYHEW
Draper James Brand Editor, *Today Show* Contributor,
and *Washington Post* Columnist

"Katie is the absolute perfect party hostess—her yummy food, gorgeous tablescapes, and fun ideas are so inspirational—but what makes her even more wonderful is how she invites her guests into her home with a warm and welcoming heart. As I thumb through this book, I can feel her hostess style radiate, and I can't wait to plan my own gatherings following all of her tips!"

—CASSIE MCCONNELL KELLEY
lifestyle expert and founder of Womanista

"I love that Katie is all about entertaining the ones you love! I'm a tried-and-true Southerner who happens to be a mom of three, and this is one of my greatest desires. Thanks, Katie, for inspiring me and so many other women who want to serve our loved ones with the best that life has to offer. I am making the lemon whoopee pies *now*!"

—HOLLY WILLIAMS
singer-songwriter and owner of White's Mercantile

"Oh, the joy and whimsy Katie has brought into the world with this beautiful book! A mix of delicious recipes, creative entertaining tips, and a heavy helping of nostalgia, her colorful words and pictures inspire us all to not only stir up a party anytime . . . but to stir up a memory. And isn't that what life is all about? To share a meal, share a memory, and inspire those around us along the way. Inspiring us to do just that, *So Much to Celebrate* has a permanent place in my kitchen."

—DAWN MCCOY
TV host, lifestyle expert, social media personality, actor, and writer

"One peek inside Katie Jacobs' book and you will be instantly transported to her lovely table. The ultimate party hostess and styling pro, Katie shares her magical gift of making entertaining look effortless—and totally doable at the same time. From the table settings at her Mother's Day tea party to the clever touches on her fall tailgating spread, I'm smitten with Katie's tips and ideas and can't wait to try them in my own home."

—ERIN BYERS MURRAY
food writer, author, and editor of *Nashville Lifestyles*

SO MUCH TO celebrate

ENTERTAINING THE ONES YOU LOVE

THE WHOLE YEAR THROUGH

KATIE JACOBS

of STYLING MY EVERYDAY

PRINCIPAL PHOTOGRAPHY *by* AMY CHERRY

THOMAS NELSON
Since 1798

Published in Nashville, Tennessee, by Thomas Nelson. Thomas Nelson is a registered trademark of HarperCollins Christian Publishing, Inc.

Thomas Nelson titles may be purchased in bulk for educational, business, fund-raising, or sales promotional use. For information, please e-mail SpecialMarkets@ThomasNelson.com.

ISBN-13: 978-0-7180-7518-7

Cover photo: Amy Cherry
Styling: Katie Jacobs
Title calligraphy: Abigail McGinnis
Cover design: Mary Hooper

Printed in China

18 19 20 21 22 DSC 10 9 8 7 6 5 4 3 2 1

CONTENTS

Fall

Winter

To my grandmother, Honey Mama,
for her love;
to my mother for her laughter;
and to my daughter, Emmaline,
who makes every day worth
celebrating.

I HAVE SO MUCH TO BE THANKFUL FOR.
THERE IS SO MUCH TO CELEBRATE!

Living life with joy and gratitude alongside the people you love makes every day special and worthy of celebration. Impromptu barefoot-in-the-kitchen dance parties, a three-tier chocolate cake just because it's Tuesday, and cotton candy–topped milkshakes to mark the end of summer vacation transform seemingly ordinary moments into the essential threads that weave together the fiber of who we are.

So many of my favorite, and profoundly pivotal, memories happened in the kitchen or around the dinner table. Eating steak and baked potatoes at the long farm table on the porch of our family's lake house, the Thanksgiving meal overflowing on my mom's kitchen island, pot roast served in my grandmother's elegant Williamsburg dining room, pizza on the floor of my first apartment—so much of my life has centered around food and sharing meals with family and friends. My grand-mother taught me how to set a table, and my mother taught me how to arrange flowers. But more importantly, they taught me the art of celebrating: how to create meaningful, unfussy gatherings—not without effort, but carried out with relative ease—that create lasting memories with the ones you love.

Now that I am a mom, I realize more and more that time is fleeting. It forces me to stop, take a breath, and remember how grateful I am that I have so much to celebrate. I want to always take the time to make loved ones feel special and create extraordinary celebrations to foster memories that will last a lifetime.

I set out to create a book that is not only beautiful but is also a guide to creating lifelong memories with your family and friends—inspiration to encourage more parties, more togetherness, more celebrations. It is my hope that the family suppers, holiday parties, and informal gatherings found in these pages will inspire you to live a little more life together with the ones you love.

spring

THE ARRIVAL OF SPRING'S FIRST SUN-KISSED DAYS BEGS TO BE CELEBRATED.

Warmer weather ushers out the long, cold days of winter, and sunny days are a welcome friend that everyone rejoices in. The season's clean slate and fresh blooms inspire parties featuring lighter menus and sunny decor. Tablescapes displaying natural elements bring the outdoors in, showcasing the earth's beautiful bounty.

There's nothing more blissful than enjoying the first flush of lovely weather with the ones you love. My favorite way to spend a springtime afternoon is with my daughter, Emmaline, at the botanical gardens, giggling and watching the geese as we sit on a vintage quilt laid in the grass. We love to pack a picnic of simple sandwiches, fresh fruit, and lemonade and bask in the sunlight for as long as possible.

Whether you're enjoying an intimate outdoor picnic for two or a porch-side dinner party for ten, spring's cheerful sun-filled days are reason enough to celebrate.

FAIRY-TALE FERN WHITE LINEN LUNCHEON

Sometimes inspiration comes in the most unexpected places. Last spring I toured a local design showhouse and noticed that nearly every designer had incorporated beautiful, lush green ferns into their spaces. Not only is greenery a simple way to breathe life into an interior, but for me, it sparked the idea for a fresh and simple spring luncheon.

Invite your girlfriends for a chic ladies' luncheon featuring relaxed white linens, fern centerpieces, and a delicate lunch to celebrate the new growth that will soon be breathing life into the long, cold days of the past winter season.

GET THE LOOK

I always try to host events that are both elegant and relaxed. In lieu of traditional plates, I used wooden paddles to serve soup and sandwiches alongside petite white macarons. Crystal candlesticks with long white tapers peeked through lush ferns planted in a collection of vintage white pitchers, and champagne was served in hardblown glass flutes. Everyone loved the watercolor and calligraphed place cards that were attached to fern branches casually draped across each place setting.

THINK OUTSIDE THE BOX

When throwing a party like this one at your own home, don't be afraid to rearrange a room or two to achieve the desired look. Change up your seating by adding a bench. Don't worry about silverware and glasses matching perfectly, and plant ferns in white containers that you already have—pitchers and colanders make for elegant and unexpected centerpieces.

Switching out art or having something new made specifically for the affair will take your party to the next level. I splurged and commissioned the watercolor and calligraphy painting "Over the River and Through the Woods" to use for the invitations. Then I framed the painting and placed it above the fireplace for the party.

THE MENU

While the decor often takes center stage, the food is what guests will really remember. Be sure to coordinate your offerings with the theme of the event. Zucchini soup with crème fraîche and cilantro, cucumber tea sandwiches with lemon and dill, vanilla bean macarons, and homemade coconut cake not only mimic the green and white decor, but will also leave your guests gushing. Paired with cucumber water, fresh green tea with mint, and champagne, toasts will abound.

ENJOY THE PARTY!

Luncheon items are super simple to make ahead. I like to set the table in advance with plates and bowls, and then during the party, when everyone is seated, I serve the warm soup to each guest by pouring it out of a pitcher. Tea sandwiches can be made the morning of, and a cake the day before. Put out beautiful glass pitchers filled with tea and water so guests can help themselves.

MAKE IT AHEAD

Prepare (or pick up) soup up to two days in advance, and reheat it on the stove the day of the party.

COCONUT CAKE

Th s recipe has become a year-round dessert that always feels appropriate for any function—snowy in the winter and light in the spring. At our wedding, in lieu of a traditional wedding cake, my husband, Brent, and I chose fourteen different 9-inch round cakes in various flavors. Each cake honored a member of our immediate family and was displayed on a tree stump or antique cake stand. The bride-and-groom's cake was a coconut cake that was adorned with my grandparents' antique cake topper. This cake (with cream cheese icing and a hint of almond extract) always takes me back to our wedding day.

1½ cups (3 sticks) unsalted butter, softened

2 cups sugar

5 large eggs, room temperature

1½ teaspoons pure vanilla extract

1½ teaspoons pure almond extract

3 cups all-purpose flour

1 teaspoon baking powder

½ teaspoon baking soda

½ teaspoon kosher salt

1 cup buttermilk

1 (14-ounce) package sweetened, shredded coconut, divided

CREAM CHEESE ICING

2 (3-ounce) packages cream cheese, softened

1½ cups (3 sticks) unsalted butter, softened

1 teaspoon pure vanilla extract

¼ teaspoon almond extract

1½ pounds powdered sugar, sifted

Makes 1 cake, approximately 12 servings

1. Preheat the oven to 350 degrees. Butter and flour three 9-inch round cake pans.
2. In the bowl of an electric mixer fitted with the paddle attachment, cream the butter and sugar on high speed until light and fluffy, about 5 minutes. With the mixer on low speed, add the eggs, one at a time, scraping down the bowl after each addition. Add the vanilla and almond extracts, and mix until just incorporated.
3. In a separate bowl sift together the flour, baking powder, baking soda, and salt. In three parts, alternately add the flour mixture and the buttermilk to the batter, beginning and ending with the flour mixture. Mix until just combined. Fold in 7 ounces of the coconut.
4. Divide the batter evenly among the three pans. Bake, rotating the pans halfway through, until golden brown and a cake tester inserted in the center comes out clean, about 25 to 35 minutes.
5. Transfer the pans to a wire rack. Once the cakes are cooled, invert them onto the racks, then reinvert, top side up. Cool completely. While the cakes are cooling, make the icing.
6. To make the cream cheese icing, in the bowl of an electric mixer fitted with the paddle attachment, on low speed cream together the cream cheese, butter, vanilla, and almond extract. Add the powdered sugar, and mix until smooth.
7. To assemble the cake, place the first layer on a serving platter. Using an offset spatula, spread the top with ¼ inch of icing. Top with the second layer, another ¼ inch of icing, and then the third layer. Ice the sides and top of the cake with the remaining icing, and cover with the remaining coconut.

MAKE IT AHEAD: Make this cake the day before serving, and store it in the refrigerator. Let it come to room temperature before serving.

BREAKFAST IN BED

Exceptional days, like birthdays and Mother's Day, require special attention. There's nothing like making breakfast in bed to show someone just how much you love him or her. It's a beautiful break from the regular routine and the perfect way to start a day of celebration.

My family loves to curl up in bed together. We usually pile in and watch a movie, or if it's someone's birthday, we all jump in together in our pj's and open early-morning gifts. On Mother's Day I'm treated to breakfast in bed that we all end up sharing. Since I'm the one who loves to cook in our house, I usually give my husband a little help by making pancake batter ahead of time so it's ready and waiting in the fridge for him. I've also been known to set out a breakfast tray the night before as a hint!

PERFECT PANCAKES

Make this pancake batter ahead of time, and store it in the refrigerator so it's ready to pour on the griddle first thing in the morning. You can also cook the pancakes, let them cool, and freeze them. That way it's easy for little hands to pop them in the toaster to heat up for a special breakfast.

2 cups all-purpose flour

1 3/4 teaspoons baking powder

1/3 cup sugar

1/2 teaspoon coarse salt

3 large eggs, separated

1 1/2 cups whole milk

6 tablespoons unsalted butter, melted, plus 1 teaspoon for cooking

1/2 teaspoon pure vanilla extract

Fresh fruit (optional)

Maple syrup

Makes approximately 18 pancakes

1. Sift the flour, baking powder, sugar, and salt into a large bowl.
2. In a medium bowl, whisk together the egg yolks, milk, 6 tablespoons butter, and vanilla until combined. Whisk the yolk mixture into the flour mixture until just combined. The batter will be slightly lumpy.
3. Place the egg whites in the bowl of an electric mixer fitted with the whisk attachment, and whisk until medium peaks form. Mix half the egg whites into the batter with a rubber spatula. Gently fold in the remaining whites. The egg whites should not be fully incorporated into the batter. Store the batter in the refrigerator in an airtight container until ready to use, or use it immediately.
4. To cook the pancakes, heat a griddle until hot, about 350 to 375 degrees. Add the remaining butter to the hot griddle. Add 1/4 cup of the pancake batter, and let it set. When bubbles begin to form, lift the pancake; if it's golden brown, turn it over. Cook until golden brown on the remaining side.
5. Transfer the cooked pancake to a plate, and keep it warm. Repeat the process with the remaining batter. Garnish with fresh fruit, and serve warm with maple syrup.

MAKE IT AHEAD: Make this batter up to a day in advance, and store it in the refrigerator in an airtight container. You can also freeze the cooked pancakes by letting them cool completely and placing them in individual freezer bags in the freezer. To cook the frozen pancakes, place them in a toaster until warmed through.

EASTER EGG HUNT

Ask me what my favorite holiday is, and *Easter* is my immediate reply. When I was a little girl, I always looked forward to wearing a new Easter dress (some years even included a matching hat), the Easter Bunny bringing baskets full of gifts and candy, and lunch at my grandmother's house, followed by an Easter egg hunt in her garden.

Easter evokes images of children loading baskets with candy-filled, pastel-colored eggs hidden in the yard, so why not host an Easter egg hunt that's all about the kids? Easter is the perfect time for family to come together to celebrate the rebirth and new life that come each spring.

GET THE LOOK

I invited friends and family over for an afternoon of sweets, and I decorated child-sized tables so the kids felt right at home. I set each place with mini Easter baskets and place cards made from handblown watercolor eggs. Kids loved finding their seats, and I sent the baskets home with each child as party favors.

Deciding on decor was easy. I wanted to celebrate the abundance of spring by decorating with bright and pastel Easter egg colors and using fresh flowers like cherry blossom branches, tulips, and daisies. I grew wheatgrass in glass containers to resemble a springtime lawn and tucked in a few speckled eggs to bring the Easter egg hunt to the dessert table.

Nowadays, most people can take high-quality photos right on their phones. Take advantage of this and put together an Easter Day photo "booth" so everyone can take pictures in their Sunday best. Use a brightly colored sheet or tablecloth as a backdrop, and decorate the edges with fresh garland and ribbon. I adore the halos made of ivy and daisies that my friend Steve McLellan made for the girls to wear for photos and during the egg hunt.

ENJOY THE PARTY!

When you're hosting a party that includes a large activity (like an Easter egg hunt), keep the menu simple. Time these events in between meal times. A midafternoon social means you don't have to plan a large menu. Sweets or light snacks will suffice. Just be sure to include an idea of what you plan to serve on the invitation so guests know what to expect and don't show up expecting a meal.

MAKE IT AHEAD

Cakes, cupcakes, and even macarons are great made in advance. Refrigerate overnight and bring to room temperature before the party.

THE MENU

I put Easter Bunny cupcakes at each place setting for the kids to dive into as soon as they arrived. Chocolate eggs held in egg-shaped candy dishes didn't last long, and a speckled hummingbird cake thrilled adults.

When we headed outside for the egg hunt, I surprised guests with extra treats—Sweet Darling Pâtisserie's Flower Cart filled with macarons. After everyone had their sugar fix and picture made, the kids ran wild collecting eggs scattered throughout the yard. Parents gathered outside as every last egg was snatched up!

If it's not in your budget to have dessert catered, make your own tiny creations and display them outside on a table topped with cake stands at varying heights. Lemon whoopie pies with lavender icing (page 44), brown butter Rice Krispies treats (page 47), and key lime coconut bars (page 93) will delight kids and adults alike.

EASTER BUNNY COCONUT CUPCAKES

These cute bunny cupcakes quickly went viral on Pinterest. One reason is because they are irresistibly adorable. The other is because they are so simple to create! To add Easter Bunny ears, pour sprinkles or colored sanding sugar into a shallow dish. Slice a marshmallow on a diagonal, and then dip the sticky sides into the sprinkles or sugar. Arrange a pair like bunny ears on top of the cupcake (the icing will act as glue). Repeat until all cupcakes are decorated. Kids will not only love eating them, but will also have great fun helping to make them!

HUMMINGBIRD CAKE

This Southern cake has become one of my family's favorite Easter traditions—maybe because it's *my* favorite and I make it each year. Isn't that how all family traditions begin? I can assure you that no one's complaining!

3 cups all-purpose flour

1 teaspoon baking soda

1 teaspoon ground cinnamon

1/2 teaspoon salt

1 cup vegetable oil

2 teaspoons pure vanilla extract

2 cups sugar

3 large eggs

2 cups mashed, ripe banana (about 3 large)

1 (8-ounce) can crushed pineapple, drained

1 cup chopped pecans

1 cup shredded coconut, unsweetened

CREAM CHEESE ICING

2 (8-ounce) packages cream cheese, softened

1 1/2 cups (3 sticks) unsalted butter, softened

1 teaspoon pure vanilla extract

1 1/2 pounds powdered sugar, sifted

Blue food coloring (optional)

SPECKLED DECORATION

1 tablespoon cocoa powder

1 1/2 tablespoons pure vanilla extract

Decorative speckled eggs (optional)

Makes 1 cake, approximately 12 servings

1. Preheat the oven to 350 degrees. Butter and flour four 8-inch round cake pans.
2. In a medium bowl whisk together the flour, baking soda, cinnamon, and salt.
3. In the bowl of an electric mixer fitted with the paddle attachment, beat the oil, vanilla, and sugar until combined, about 2 minutes. Add the eggs one at a time, incorporating each before adding the next. Beat at medium speed until the mixture is pale yellow and fluffy, about 3 minutes.
4. In a separate bowl mix together the banana, pineapple, pecans, and coconut. Add to the egg mixture, and stir until well combined. Add the flour mixture, and blend well.
5. Divide the batter evenly among the pans. Bake, rotating the pans halfway through, until the cakes are golden brown and a cake tester inserted in the center comes out clean, about 25 to 35 minutes.
6. Transfer the pans to a wire rack. Once the cakes are cooled, invert them onto the racks, then reinvert them so they are top side up. Cool completely. While the cakes are cooling, make the icing.
7. To make the icing, in the bowl of an electric mixer fitted with the paddle attachment, on low speed cream together the cream cheese, butter, and vanilla. Add the powdered sugar, and mix until smooth. Divide the icing evenly between two bowls. Add 2 to 3 drops of blue food coloring, if using, to one bowl of icing, and mix until the color is evenly distributed (add one drop at a time until you reach the desired shade).
8. To assemble the cake, place a layer on a serving platter. Using an offset spatula, spread the layer with 1/4 inch of white icing. Top with the next layer, and repeat the process until all four layers are stacked. Ice the sides and top of the cake with the remaining white icing to create a crumb coat. Refrigerate the cake until the icing is set. Ice the sides and top of cake with blue buttercream, and smooth it using a warm metal spatula.
9. To make the speckled decoration, in a small bowl mix together the cocoa powder and vanilla. Stir well until the cocoa is completely dissolved and the consistency is like thin chocolate paint. Cover your work area with wax paper. Lightly dip a basting brush or new paintbrush into the chocolate. Holding the brush with one hand, gently flick the bristles with your other index finger to splatter the chocolate paint. Practice first on your wax paper until you get the hang of it. When you're ready to start speckling, hold the paintbrush fairly close to the cake, and start splattering. Move up, down, and all around to completely cover the cake. Top the cake with decorative eggs.

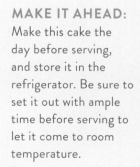

MAKE IT AHEAD:
Make this cake the day before serving, and store it in the refrigerator. Be sure to set it out with ample time before serving to let it come to room temperature.

MAKE IT AHEAD:
Make macarons
ahead of time, and
freeze them in an
airtight container for
up to three months.
Let them defrost for
at least 20 minutes
before serving.

SARAH DARLING'S TIFFANY VANILLA MACARONS

Just like my friend Sarah Darling, these French macarons are beautiful inside and out. These petite, brightly colored confections are the perfect creations of her dessert business, Sweet Darling Pâtisserie. Don't feel intimidated about making macarons at home! Just follow Sarah's advice: "Be sure not to overmix your batter, don't bake on a rainy day, and practice makes perfect!"

1¼ cups almond flour

1¼ cups powdered sugar

3 egg whites, room temperature

⅓ cup superfine sugar

½ teaspoon pure vanilla extract

Blue food coloring

VANILLA BUTTERCREAM

½ cup (1 stick) unsalted butter, softened

2 cups powdered sugar, sifted

2 tablespoons heavy cream

1½ teaspoons pure vanilla extract

1 vanilla bean, seeds scraped

Makes 20 macarons

1. Preheat the oven to 300 degrees. Line two baking sheets with baking mats or parchment paper.
2. In the bowl of a food processor, combine the almond flour and powdered sugar. Pulse several times. Remove the mixture from the food processor, and sift it into a large bowl.
3. In the bowl of an electric mixer fitted with the whisk attachment, beat the egg whites on high speed. After about 20 seconds, turn the mixer to low and add the superfine sugar and vanilla. Return to high speed and beat for 6 minutes. After 6 minutes, add the food coloring one drop at a time, beating after each drop until the desired color is achieved and the color is even throughout the batter.
4. Remove the bowl from the mixer, and add the flour mixture all at once. Fold in the flour mixture with a rubber spatula until a smooth batter forms (the batter should look like ribbons coming off your spoon).
5. Transfer the mixture to a piping bag, and use a ¼-inch plain round tip to pipe 1¼-inch circles 1 inch apart, trying to keep them all the same size. Once all are piped, tap the baking sheet against the counter a couple times to release any air bubbles.
6. Leave the macarons at room temperature to dry for about 15 to 20 minutes until the tops have dulled. Bake on the bottom rack of the oven for approximately 10 minutes until set but not browned, opening the door once or twice to rotate the pan and let out steam (this prevents the macarons from cracking). Remove the pans from the oven and allow the macarons to cool.
7. While the macarons are cooling, prepare the vanilla buttercream. In the bowl of an electric mixer fitted with the paddle attachment, cream together the butter and sugar on medium speed. Once smooth, reduce the speed, and add the cream and the vanilla extract and seeds. Mix on medium speed until smooth.
8. Spoon the mixture into a clean piping bag. Pipe or spread the filling on the flat sides of half of the cookies; top them with the remaining half. Wrap the macarons in plastic and refrigerate.

MOTHER'S DAY TEA PARTY

When I was growing up, my grandmother (whom we affectionately called "Honey Mama") would host tiny tea parties in her kitchen for my cousins and me. They were miniature versions of the grand elegance that she would create on her dining room table—set with the finest china, silver, and crystal. We would dress up in her costume jewelry and snack on cookies and sandwiches, pretending to be at the most elaborate of parties. So many of my childhood memories were made at that tiny table in Honey Mama's kitchen.

Now that I'm a mom, I want to pass along those sweet memories and traditions to my children. One Mother's Day I invited four generations to a tea party to celebrate the strong women in my family. We gathered around a table set with my grandmother's china and crystal (that has now been passed on to me) and traded old stories of those childhood tea parties. My ninety-four-year-old grandmother and my mother were touched by the affair, and we all loved watching my daughter, Emmaline, enjoy her very first tea party.

You don't have to be a *Downton Abbey* devotee to appreciate the charm and elegance of an English-style tea party. A tea party is a wonderfully feminine celebration where elegant finger foods being passed around the table, tea being poured from a silver service, and spring flowers bursting in their brightness all set the scene for conversation and laughter.

GET THE LOOK

Let the decor be a celebration of your family. I love using heirloom pieces that have been passed down through generations. I'm a fourth-generation Nashvillian, so I asked my friend Abi McGinnis to hand-letter napkins with sayings that Southern mothers always seem to say, like "Bless your heart" and "Suck it up, buttercup." For party favors, I monogrammed hankies with everyone's initials as a lasting memory of the day. Paper butterflies perched on water glasses served as place cards, and silver picture frames filled with old photos of mother and daughter were sent home with each mom as a Mother's Day gift.

MAKE IT AHEAD

Set the table the day before, and assemble the tiered stands with food the morning of the party.

THE MENU

Yes, it's all about the tea, but it's the food that will bring your guests the most delight. Tiered stands of decadent desserts, tiny sandwiches, and pastries spark thoughts of Marie Antoinette. Have the meal catered or make the food yourself, but tea sandwiches, scones, macarons, shortbread, fruit tarts, petit fours, Linzer cookies, and madeleines are musts. When the party is over, pack up leftover tea sandwiches and sweets in bakery boxes for everyone to enjoy later.

ENJOY THE PARTY!

When it comes to an extravagant party like this one, *more is more*. I really wanted cake stands *overflowing* with treats. Be realistic, though, about your time and abilities. I had most of the food for this event catered because I wanted such a vast variety of items that personally making them all just wasn't feasible.

20

CUCUMBER TEA SANDWICHES WITH LEMON AND DILL

Tea sandwiches are a must for any tea party! This recipe is light and fresh, making it the perfect finger food.

8 ounces whipped cream cheese

1/3 cup roughly chopped fresh dill

2 teaspoons freshly squeezed lemon juice

1 teaspoon finely chopped lemon zest

1/4 teaspoon salt

Pinch of freshly ground black pepper

1 large English cucumber

12 to 16 slices good-quality white sandwich bread

Makes 12 to 16 tea sandwiches

1. Place the cream cheese in a bowl, and stir with a spoon or fork until smooth and free of lumps. Add the dill, lemon juice, lemon zest, salt, and pepper, and stir until well combined. Chill the cream cheese mixture for approximately 2 hours (or overnight) to allow the flavors to meld.
2. To prepare the sandwiches, allow the cream cheese mixture to sit at room temperature for approximately 30 minutes until it becomes easily spreadable. Thinly slice the cucumber into rounds using a mandoline or a sharp knife.
3. Using two slices of bread, spread a thin layer of the cream cheese mixture onto each slice, and arrange the cucumber slices (just touching one another) on top of one slice. Top with the other slice of bread, and trim away the bread crusts with a serrated knife. Then cut the sandwiches into desired shapes (2 triangles or 2 rectangles). Serve immediately, or layer in an airtight container with waxed paper between each layer and on top of the top layer. Refrigerate the sandwiches until you are ready to serve them. Ideally, cucumber tea sandwiches should be served within about 2 to 3 hours after they are assembled.

MAKE IT AHEAD: While the sandwiches need to be assembled the day of the party, you can make the spread and slice the cucumber the day before.

BRIDES WHO BRUNCH

The celebrations surrounding a wedding are memorable occasions that not only honor the bride and groom, but also delight loved ones whom the couple holds dear. Bridal showers are the perfect opportunity to up the girlie factor, and choosing a theme is imperative. A bridal brunch or afternoon tea is a perfect get-together for ladies to socialize and shower the bride with love and gifts.

Brunch is an especially easy affair to pull together. Creating a menu of brunch favorites like scones, waffles, and donuts is fun. Guests are usually available and happy to attend a late-morning event, and they won't arrive starved (like they would if you were serving lunch).

When my cousin Julianna got married, we threw her a bakery-themed bridesmaids' brunch decorated with hot-pink bakery boxes and garden roses. We invited guests by hand-delivering bakery boxes filled with cupcakes and mini macarons with the brunch invitations attached. Then for the party we decorated a long farm table with pink bakery boxes, vintage cake stands, and hot-pink garden roses.

Brunch consisted of ham and cheese croissants, mini frittatas, and fruit and granola parfaits served in pink Depression glass bowls. Guests enjoyed homemade cranberry-orange and Cheddar-dill scones served with mimosas, tea, and coffee. We repurposed the bakery boxes used as decorations to pack up the leftover baked goods and send them home with guests as favors.

HAM AND SWISS CROISSANTS WITH POPPY-SEED MUSTARD

3/4 cup (1 1/2 sticks) butter, melted, divided

1 1/2 tablespoons Dijon mustard

1 1/2 teaspoons Worcestershire sauce

12 croissants

1 pound thinly sliced Swiss cheese

1 pound thinly sliced deli ham

1 1/2 tablespoons poppy seeds

Makes 12 sandwiches

1. Preheat the oven to 350 degrees. Line a rimmed baking sheet with parchment paper.
2. In a bowl mix together 1/2 cup of the butter, the Dijon, and the Worcestershire. Slice the croissants, separating the tops from the bottoms. Layer the ham on the bottom of the croissants, then arrange the Swiss cheese over the ham. Slather the sliced-side of each croissant top with mustard sauce, place the tops of the croissants onto the sandwiches, and place the sandwiches on the baking sheet (they can be put close together, even touching, on the baking sheet). Pour the remaining melted butter evenly over each croissant, and sprinkle with poppy seeds.
3. Bake until the croissants are browned and the cheese has melted, about 10 to 12 minutes. If the tops start to get too brown, cover with aluminum foil. Serve warm or at room temperature.

SPRING MENU

By the time spring arrives, everyone is looking for lighter, healthier options to break the routine of comforting winter casseroles. It's time to crank up the grill and invite friends over to enjoy the new season with warmer days and still-cool evenings.

Our Saturday mornings consist of my favorite family activity: going to the farmers' market. We stroll across the street, and people laugh and "aww" as Emmaline eats tomatoes like apples, with juice running down her face, arms, and shirt. Our stroller looks like a pack mule loaded down with a huge basket of CSA vegetables, boxes of donuts, glasses of fresh lemonade, bags of fresh pasta, and baskets of berries. I spend the rest of the afternoon washing vegetables, stocking our fridge, and planning our meals for the week.

Your local farmers' market is the best place to get not only fresh, seasonal produce and meat, but also ideas and inspiration for family meals. I usually go to the market with no plans, buy whatever looks beautiful, then go home and create a meal around it.

- Gluten-Free Lemon Ricotta Pancakes

- The Ultimate Skinny Margarita

- Spiked Pomegranate Mint Lemonade

- Grilled Avocados with Pico de Gallo

- Turkey Burgers

- Chicken Tortilla Soup

- Deviled Eggs with Bacon Jam

- Lemon Blueberry Tart

- Lemon Whoopie Pies with Lavender Icing

- E Bear's Brown Butter Rice Krispies Treats

GLUTEN-FREE LEMON RICOTTA PANCAKES

When entertaining you want to be sure to cater to your guests, and being aware of food allergies is part of being a gracious host. I developed this gluten-free pancake recipe when I was hosting a group for breakfast and knew a couple of the guests were gluten intolerant. These pancakes are so delicious that everyone will love them, whether they can eat gluten or not. The recipe uses a gluten-free baking mix to cut out any guesswork. Lucky for everyone, champagne is gluten free, so mimosas all around!

3 arge eggs, separated

3 tablespoons sugar, divided

Zest of 2 lemons

1 tablespoon pure vanilla extract

5 tablespoons butter, melted

1 cup milk

2 cups gluten-free pancake mix

3/4 cup ricotta cheese

Pomegranate arils, maple syrup, powdered sugar, and/or lemon zest for garnish

Makes 12 pancakes

1. In the bowl of an electric mixer fitted with the whisk attachment, beat the egg whites until they start to bubble. Sprinkle in 1 tablespoon of the sugar, and continue beating until soft peaks form.
2. In a large bowl beat with a whisk the egg yolks, remaining 2 tablespoons sugar, lemon zest, and vanilla. Beat in the butter and milk until smooth. Add the pancake mix, and stir with a rubber spatula until just combined (do not overmix). Fold the whipped egg whites into the batter until just combined. Gently fold the ricotta cheese into the batter. The batter will be lumpy.
3. Heat a nonstick skillet over medium heat. Pour 3 to 4 tablespoons of the batter onto the skillet. Once little bubbles form, turn and continue to cook until the pancake is evenly browned on each side. Repeat with the remaining batter.
4. Serve the pancakes with your choice of fruit, maple syrup, powdered sugar, and/or lemon zest.

MAKE IT AHEAD: Make this batter the day before, and store it in the refrigerator in an airtight container.

THE ULTIMATE SKINNY MARGARITA

This is my favorite margarita because it's incredibly fresh and happens to be low calorie. It's always a hit at parties, and I have written down the recipe countless times to send home with inquiring guests. Put out a tray with limes and salt so guests can rim their own glasses since some like more salt and others like less.

Kosher salt

Lime slices or wedges

1½ cups white tequila

¾ cup light agave syrup

¾ cup freshly squeezed lime juice (about 6 limes)

Makes 6 margaritas

1. To rim the glass, pour some kosher salt into a small dish. Rub 1 lime slice over half the rim of an Old Fashioned glass. Dip the rim of the glass into the salt, then fill the glass with ice. Repeat with additional glasses.
2. In a large cocktail shaker or Mason jar, combine the tequila, agave syrup, and lime juice. Fill with ice and shake well, then strain into prepared glasses. Garnish with a fresh lime slice.

Note: You can turn this margarita into a summer-friendly slushie by pureeing it in a blender with 2 cups of ice.

MAKE IT AHEAD: Slice and juice your limes a day in advance. Wait until just before guests arrive to mix the pitcher of margaritas.

SPIKED POMEGRANATE MINT LEMONADE

Serving a signature cocktail for any event is always a fun idea. I made this spiked lemonade for a staycation we took to Leiper's Fork, Tennessee. We booked the most adorable cabin, called Storybook Cottage, for the night and invited a handful of friends to join us for dinner by the fire. I premade enchiladas (recipe on page 145), key lime pie, and this spiked lemonade. It's incredibly simple to put together and is the perfect light, refreshing cocktail for spring and summer.

½ cup fresh mint, packed

1 cup sugar

8 cups water, divided

Juice of 6 lemons

2 cups vodka

Ice cubes

Pomegranate juice (optional)

Fresh lemon slices and fresh mint for garnish

Makes 8 to 10 servings

1. To make the mint-infused simple syrup, roughly tear or chop mint leaves in half. Combine the sugar, 1 cup of the water, and the mint leaves in a saucepan over a medium heat, stirring gently and constantly until the sugar is dissolved. Remove the syrup from the heat and let it cool completely. Using a fine mesh strainer, strain the mint leaves out of the simple syrup and transfer it to a sterilized airtight container. Use the syrup immediately, or store it in the refrigerator for up to 1 month.

2. To make the drink, in a pitcher or drink dispenser, combine the syrup, the remaining 7 cups of water, lemon juice, vodka, and ice, and stir to combine. Add a splash of pomegranate juice, if using, and garnish with lemon slices and fresh mint.

MAKE IT AHEAD: Make the mint-infused simple syrup, and store it in the refrigerator for up to one month. Slice and juice the lemons a day in advance, and make the lemonade just before guests arrive.

GRILLED AVOCADOS WITH PICO DE GALLO

When it comes to grilling fruits and veggies, I like to think outside the box—grilling eggplant, whole Vidalia onions, or even peaches. One of my very favorite foods to grill has to be avocados. Sliced in half, brushed with lime juice, and topped with pico de gallo, they are bound to become your new favorite as well. Plus, they sure make for an impressive presentation!

4 ripe avocados, pitted and halved

Juice of 2 limes, divided

Olive oil

Salt and freshly ground black pepper to taste

1 medium tomato, diced

1 onion, finely chopped

½ jalapeño pepper, seeded and chopped

2 sprigs fresh cilantro, finely chopped

Makes 8 servings

1. Set the outdoor grill to medium-high heat.
2. Brush the avocado halves with the lime juice, reserving 1 tablespoon, and then brush them with the olive oil. Sprinkle with salt and pepper. Place the avocados flesh side down on the hot grill over indirect heat for 5 to 7 minutes until grill marks are visible.
3. Make the pico de gallo by tossing together the tomato, onion, jalapeño, cilantro, and the remaining 1 tablespoon of lime juice. Season with salt and pepper to taste.
4. Remove the avocados from the grill, and fill each pit hole with pico de gallo.

MAKE IT AHEAD: Make the pico de gallo up to two days in advance. Grill the avocados just before serving.

TURKEY BURGERS

When the weather starts getting warmer, I get the itch to crank up the grill. These turkey burgers are easy enough for weeknight family meals and are a healthy option for neighborhood get-togethers.

1 tablespoon olive oil, plus more for grilling

1/2 medium sweet onion, diced small

2 minced garlic cloves

1/4 cup bread crumbs

1 tablespoon whole-grain mustard

1/4 cup finely chopped parsley

11/4 pounds (20 ounces) ground turkey

Salt and freshly ground black pepper

Provolone cheese (optional)

Pretzel buns

Desired toppings

Makes 4 burgers

1. In a medium skillet heat the oil over medium heat. Add the onion and sauté until translucent (not brown), about 4 to 5 minutes. Add the garlic and cook until fragrant, about 1 minute (being careful not to burn the garlic).
2. Transfer the onion and garlic to a medium bowl, and allow to cool slightly. To the onion mixture add the bread crumbs, mustard, and parsley, and stir until well mixed. Add the ground turkey, and gently mix with your hands or a fork until just combined.
3. Form 4 patties, slightly larger in diameter than the hamburger buns, as the patties will shrink as they cook. Arrange the patties on a plate using parchment paper to separate the patties. Refrigerate them until you are ready to grill them.
4. Heat a grill or grill pan to medium-high heat. Clean and lightly oil the hot grill. Season the patties with salt and pepper, then brush with oil. Grill the patties, covered, until they are cooked through, about 4 to 6 minutes per side. During the last minute of cooking, top each burger with cheese, if using, and cover the grill until the cheese is melted.
5. Serve the burgers on buns with desired toppings.

MAKE IT AHEAD: Make the uncooked turkey burger patties up to two days in advance, and store them in the refrigerator in an airtight container.

CHICKEN TORTILLA SOUP

This simple one-pot supper can be made in less than an hour. Using a rotisserie chicken from the grocery store helps cut down on prep work, while throwing in fire-roasted tomatoes and chargrilled whole wheat tortillas adds a great smoky flavor. Offer your favorite toppings, such as sour cream, avocado, lime zest, queso fresco, and even pomegranate arils so guests can customize their own bowls of soup.

2 tablespoons vegetable oil

1 cup diced onion

¼ cup diced red bell pepper

¼ cup diced green bell pepper

3 cloves garlic, minced

2 jalapeño peppers, finely diced

1 teaspoon ground cumin

½ teaspoon salt

5 cups low-sodium chicken broth

1 cup water, plus additional for cornmeal

1 (14.5-ounce) can fire-roasted diced tomatoes

1 (14.5-ounce) can black beans, rinsed and drained

1 rotisserie chicken, meat removed and shredded

3 tablespoons cornmeal

Juice of 2 limes, plus wedges for garnish

½ cup roughly chopped fresh cilantro leaves

Salt and freshly ground black pepper

5 (8-inch) flour tortillas (I like to use whole wheat), charred or grilled, cut into thin strips

Optional assorted toppings: lime wedges and zest, avocado, queso fresco, grilled tortilla strips or tortilla chips, sour cream, pomegranate arils

Makes 6 servings

1. In a large pot or Dutch oven heat the vegetable oil over medium heat. Add the onions and red and green peppers, and cook for 2 minutes. Once the onions and peppers have softened, add the garlic, jalapeños, cumin, and salt, and cook for another minute.
2. Pour the chicken broth, water, tomatoes, and beans into the pot, and bring to a boil. Once at a boil, lower the heat to simmer, and add the shredded chicken. Cook for 20 to 25 minutes.
3. In a small bowl mix the cornmeal with a small amount of water. Pour into the soup, then simmer for an additional 30 minutes.
4. Add the lime juice and fresh cilantro to the pot, and season with salt and pepper to taste. Add the tortilla strips to the soup 5 to 10 minutes before serving.
5. Ladle the soup into serving bowls, and top with desired garnishes—a lime wedge, lime zest, avocado slices, cheese, tortilla chips, sour cream, and pomegranate arils.

MAKE IT AHEAD: Except for the tortilla strips, this soup can be made a day in advance. Make the soup, allow it to cool completely, and refrigerate it in an airtight container. When you are ready to serve, return it to medium heat, stirring frequently until the soup is hot. Add in the charred flour tortilla strips 5 to 10 minutes before serving.

DEVILED EGGS WITH BACON JAM

My great-aunt Violet used to make deviled eggs for every family get-together. My dad still talks about snatching one out of the refrigerator before lunch was served! You can bet we've carried on the tradition and have deviled eggs at every family function (especially Easter). I prefer a classic deviled egg with a spectacular topping. Basically, these deviled eggs are just carriers for a ridiculously delicious bacon jam. I think Aunt Vitty would approve.

6 large eggs, hard-boiled and peeled

1/4 cup mayonnaise

1 1/2 tablespoons sweet pickle relish

1 teaspoon yellow mustard

Salt and freshly ground black pepper to taste

Smoked paprika to taste

Bacon Jam (recipe below)

Makes 12 deviled eggs

BACON JAM

3/4 pound quality thick-sliced bacon, cut crosswise into 1-inch pieces

1 medium yellow onion, diced small

2 garlic cloves, minced

1/4 cup apple cider vinegar

1/4 cup packed dark brown sugar

2 tablespoons real maple syrup

6 tablespoons brewed coffee

Makes 1 cup

1. Halve the eggs lengthwise. Remove the yolks and place in a small bowl.
2. Mash the yolks with a fork, and stir in the mayonnaise, pickle relish, and mustard. Add salt, pepper, and paprika to taste.
3. Use a piping bag to fill the egg whites evenly with the yolk mixture. Garnish with paprika and bacon jam. Store covered in the refrigerator.
4. To make the jam, in a large skillet cook the bacon over medium heat until the fat is rendered and the bacon is lightly browned, about 2 minutes. With a slotted spoon, transfer the bacon to a paper towel.
5. Pour off the excess oil from the pan, and add the onions and garlic. Cook over medium heat until the onions are translucent, about 5 minutes (be careful not to burn the garlic). Add the vinegar, brown sugar, maple syrup, and coffee. Bring the mixture to a boil, stirring frequently. Add the cooked bacon, and stir to combine. Cook on low for 20 to 30 minutes until thickened.
6. Remove the jam from the heat, allow it to cool, and store it in the refrigerator in an airtight container for up to four weeks.

Tip: To easily hard-boil eggs, use older eggs, as they are easier to peel, so let them sit in your refrigerator for at least a week before you boil them. Put the eggs in a single layer in a large saucepan. Cover with at least an inch of cold water (this prevents cracking). Add 1/2 teaspoon of salt and 1 tablespoon of vinegar. Bring the eggs to a boil over high heat. Boil for 30 seconds, turn off the burner, and remove the pan from the heat. Cover the pan with a tight lid, and leave (off the heat) for 12 minutes. Remove the eggs with a slotted spoon, and place them in a bowl of ice water to stop the cooking.

Note: If you prefer a smoother consistency, after the jam has cooked and thickened, transfer the warm jam to a food processor and pulse until coarsely chopped. Then allow the jam to cool before storing it in the refrigerator.

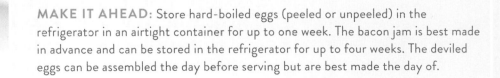

MAKE IT AHEAD: Store hard-boiled eggs (peeled or unpeeled) in the refrigerator in an airtight container for up to one week. The bacon jam is best made in advance and can be stored in the refrigerator for up to four weeks. The deviled eggs can be assembled the day before serving but are best made the day of.

LEMON BLUEBERRY TART

My mom is a chocoholic, but there is something about this lemon tart that makes her go weak in the knees. I have served it on countless occasions, and when I present it, people don't seem all that excited. While it is beautiful, I think most underestimate the power of a really good lemon tart. But after a big meal, it's the perfect smooth, fresh, not-too-sweet dessert that everyone ends up gushing over . . . Every. Single. Time.

SHORTBREAD CRUST

1 cup (2 sticks) unsalted butter, softened

1/2 cup powdered sugar

3 cups all-purpose flour

1/4 teaspoon baking powder

FILLING AND TOPPING

1 cup sugar

3 tablespoons cornstarch

1 cup whole milk

3 large egg yolks, beaten

1/4 cup (1/2 stick) butter

1 tablespoon fresh lemon zest (about 1 lemon), plus additional for garnish

1/4 cup freshly squeezed lemon juice (about 2 lemons)

8 ounces sour cream

2 cups fresh blueberries, washed and allowed to dry, divided

Fresh whipped cream (optional)

Makes 1 tart

1. Preheat the oven to 350 degrees.
2. To make the crust, in the bowl of an electric mixer fitted with the paddle attachment, cream the butter and sugar until the mixture is light and fluffy. In a separate bowl whisk together the flour and baking powder. Mix the flour mixture into the butter with the mixer on low until dough forms. Pat the dough into a buttered 9-inch tart pan. Bake for 12 to 15 minutes until lightly golden brown. Let the crust cool completely.
3. To make the filling, in a saucepan over medium heat, whisk together the sugar and cornstarch. Immediately add the milk, egg yolks, butter, and lemon zest, whisking well while adding each to avoid clumps. Cook the mixture, whisking constantly, until it thickens and begins to bubble. Continue cooking and whisking for 2 minutes. Remove the pan from the heat, and whisk in the lemon juice.
4. Let the filling cool to room temperature. Pour it into the crust, and refrigerate the tart for at least 30 minutes.
5. In a medium bowl fold together sour cream and 1 1/2 cups of the blueberries. Spread the sour cream and blueberry mixture on top of the lemon curd. Keep the topping refrigerated until you are ready to serve.
6. Top with fresh whipped cream, the remaining 1/2 cup of blueberries, and lemon zest just before serving.

MAKE IT AHEAD: This lemon tart can be made up to a day in advance, except for the whipped cream topping. The fresh whipped cream will need to be made just before serving and added to the top of the tart along with the blueberries and lemon zest.

LEMON WHOOPIE PIES WITH LAVENDER ICING

Several years ago I was hired to photograph a pie book for an Amish author. In about five weeks, I tested, cooked, styled, and photographed more than one hundred pies. Whew! The project was overwhelming and an amazing experience. From it, I learned about Amish whoopie pies—a traditional Amish dessert consisting of two soft cookies with a fluffy white filling. After the book wrapped, I came up with this lemon version with just a hint of lavender in the filling, creating a sweet, delicate confection with intricate commingling flavors.

1½ cups all-purpose flour

1 teaspoon baking powder

½ teaspoon baking soda

½ teaspoon salt

6 tablespoons unsalted butter, softened

1 cup white sugar

1 teaspoon lemon zest

1 large egg

1 tablespoon freshly squeezed lemon juice

1 teaspoon pure vanilla extract

½ cup buttermilk

LAVENDER ICING

6 tablespoons unsalted butter, softened

6 ounces cream cheese, softened

1 teaspoon pure vanilla extract

1 tablespoon freshly squeezed lemon juice

6 to 8 drops pure lavender extract

3 cups powdered sugar, plus extra for dusting

Makes 12 to 15 whoopie pies

1. Preheat the oven to 350 degrees. Line two baking sheets with baking mats or parchment paper.
2. In a medium bowl whisk together the flour, baking powder, baking soda, and salt.
3. In the bowl of a mixer fitted with the paddle attachment, beat the butter and sugar on medium speed until the mixture is light and fluffy. Add the lemon zest, egg, lemon juice, and vanilla, and mix until smooth. Reduce the speed to low, and add the flour mixture and buttermilk, alternating the flour mixture and buttermilk, starting and ending with the flour mixture, until the ingredients are just combined.
4. Transfer the mixture to a pastry bag, with ½ inch cut off the tip. Pipe 1-inch rounds about 2 inches apart on the prepared baking sheets.
5. Bake for 10 to 12 minutes until a toothpick inserted into the center comes out clean. Remove the pans from the oven, and place on baking sheets until the cookies are completely cool.
6. To make the icing, in the bowl of an electric mixer fitted with the whisk attachment beat the butter and cream cheese on medium speed until smooth. Add the vanilla and lemon juice. Add the lavender, tasting after every couple drops until there is a light lavender taste. Add the powdered sugar, and mix until smooth. Transfer the icing to a pastry bag, and cut ½ inch off the tip.
7. Turn one cooled cookie upside down, flat side facing up. Pipe icing on top of the flat side of the cookie, then place another cookie, flat side down, on top of the filling, then sandwich together. Repeat with all cookies. Dust each cookie with sifted powdered sugar. Store in the refrigerator in an airtight container, and serve within 24 hours.

E BEAR'S BROWN BUTTER RICE KRISPIES TREATS

My daughter, Emmaline, nicknamed "E Bear" by her daddy, loves to help me cook. She demands to be placed on the counter with her own mixing bowl and spoon and, of course, taste-test everything. If she hears the mixer turn on, she literally comes running so she doesn't miss a baking opportunity. Her favorite thing to make (or should I say eat!) are these Rice Krispies treats. Now, don't be fooled—just because they can be made with the assistance of a toddler doesn't mean they aren't spectacular. The perfect combination of sweet and salty, gooey and crunchy will make any child or adult swoon.

6 tablespoons butter

10 cups mini marshmallows, divided

6 cups Rice Krispies cereal

1/2 teaspoon salt

Makes 16 squares

1. Line a 9 x 9-inch pan with wax paper, and spray lightly with cooking spray.
2. Brown the butter by melting it in a large saucepan over medium heat. Use a pan with a light-colored bottom so you can keep track of the butter color. Swirl the pan occasionally to be sure the butter is cooking evenly.
3. As the butter melts, it will begin to foam. The color will progress from lemony yellow to golden tan and finally to a toasty brown. Once the butter has a nutty aroma, turn the heat to low and add in 8 cups of mini marshmallows, stirring constantly.
4. Once the marshmallows are just melted, remove them from the heat and stir in the cereal and salt until the cereal is just coated with the marshmallow mixture. Then stir in the remaining 2 cups of mini marshmallows.
5. Pour the mixture into the prepared pan, and press evenly. (Use a piece of plastic wrap sprayed lightly with cooking spray to help press the mixture into the pan, if needed.)
6. Allow the treats to cool completely. Then lift the entire square out of the pan by pulling up on the wax paper, and slice it into squares. These are best served the same day.

Summer

IT'S TIME TO RELAX AND ENJOY THE BEST OF SUMMER'S BREEZY DAYS AND BALMY NIGHTS.

My childhood summers were filled with family trips to our lake house on Center Hill Lake. Freckled-faced, I'd strap on my life jacket and reluctantly jump into the cold water that first weekend of summer bliss. After a morning of tubing and skiing with my brother behind my dad's ski boat, we would meet my grandparents on their pontoon boat to eat lunch tucked under the shade trees. Cold fried chicken, fresh fruit, and egg salad, passed from boat to boat, were quickly gobbled up before the adults started a game of Rook and the kids jumped off the sides of the boat, swimming under the pontoons. Following an afternoon of sun, we would grab ice cream at the boat dock before heading back to the house to cook dinner and eat out on the screened-in porch.

Oh, sweet summertime! A carefree season that embraces unfussy, effortless entertaining full of bright colors, bare feet, and wet swimsuits. Make the great outdoors your dining room, and take advantage of the extra daylight hours by hosting casual al fresco meals with family and friends.

FOURTH OF JULY POOL PARTY

When Independence Day arrives and the weather is hot, there's no better place to enjoy the spoils of summer than by the pool. Adults and children alike slip into their swimsuits and take a dip in the cool water for fun family memories that last a lifetime.

Throughout the summer we take full advantage of my parents' beautiful pool. To say Emmaline is a water baby is an understatement—romps through the sprinkler fill our weekends, and for my fearless child, diving headfirst into the pool has never been anything but sheer joy.

By the time the Fourth of July rolls around, summer is at its peak, and I'm in party mode—ready to celebrate not only the season but also an America that has afforded us the opportunity and freedom to do so.

GET THE LOOK

Invite friends over for poolside fun late in the afternoon when the intense heat of the day begins to die down. No need to worry with a bunch of fussy decorations; let the pool be the star. Be sure to put out fresh towels for guests, and always appoint a designated adult to watch swimmers.

For this Fourth of July celebration, I combined brightly colored summer decor with traditional red, white, and blue for a super fun update. I displayed food outside on a blue-and-white gingham tablecloth, hung paper lanterns under colorful umbrellas, and stuck handfuls of American flags into potted plants. Mason jars made for great relaxed glassware, red bandanas served as napkins, and blue-and-white enamel plates were beautiful (and, more importantly, unbreakable) serviceware.

If you don't have access to a pool, don't sweat it! Use inflatable pools and a sprinkler to create a homemade splash pad for the kids. Turn on a bubble machine and some music, and let kids play while the adults socialize. Or, if you have a yard with a hill, use a tarp to make an oversized slip-n-slide and watch the adults beg the kids for a turn.

THE MENU

We ditched the traditional burgers and hot dogs for a more sophisticated (but still unfussy) menu. Tomato, mozzarella, and arugula pizzas with prosciutto and a balsamic glaze were irresistible served alongside mini Caesar salads topped with homemade Parmesan crackers. Watermelon wedges were made handheld by adding mini Popsicle sticks and then drizzled with fresh lime juice, chopped mint, and sea salt. I made a big batch of fresh lemonade for the group and cucumber watermelon margaritas for the adults.

MAKE IT AHEAD

Keep things cool and casual with a premade frozen dessert. Popsicles and ice cream are quick crowd-pleasers.

ENJOY THE PARTY!

Don't feel like everything has to be homemade all the time. Store-bought or catered treats can be a great stress reliever for the host. It's all about the presentation—making sure that anything store-bought matches the look of the rest of the party.

For this party, in lieu of making dessert, I surprised guests mid-party with a gelato cart from Nashville's Legato Gelato. Owner Terri-Ann served up mango and strawberry sorbetto alongside dark chocolate and Madagascar bourbon vanilla gelato on sugar cones. For summertime parties like this, I also like to include throwback Popsicles and ice cream novelties (think Bomb Pops, strawberry shortcake ice cream bars, and ice cream sandwiches) and serve them in a galvanized tub of ice. These are always instant hits with the adults, who love reminiscing about their own childhood favorites.

When dusk arrived, I set out vintage enamel buckets filled with sand and sparklers plus bubbles for kids who were too young for fireworks. Long red, white, and blue tubes of bubbles also served as party favors for the little ones to make leaving the pool a little less upsetting!

CUCUMBER WATERMELON MARGARITAS

This cocktail recipe is a little labor intensive (slicing, juicing, and straining the watermelon and cucumber) but totally worth it. It gives a fresh spin to a traditional margarita by adding the quintessential flavors of sweet summertime.

8 cups seedless watermelon chunks, plus wedges for garnish

1/2 English cucumber, coarsely chopped

Zest of 1 lime, plus juice of 1/2 lime and wedges for rimming glasses

1/4 cup kosher salt

1 ounce agave syrup or honey

3 ounces white tequila

Mint sprigs for garnish

Makes 1 margarita, plus additional watermelon-cucumber juice

1. Liquefy the watermelon and cucumber in a blender, and then strain the juice through a fine-mesh strainer into a pitcher. Refrigerate the pitcher until you are ready to make the margaritas. You will not need all the watermelon and cucumber juice.
2. Mix the lime zest and salt on a small plate.
3. When it's time to serve, mix 1/2 cup watermelon-cucumber juice with the lime juice, agave, and tequila in a cocktail shaker filled with ice. Shake well to chill.
4. Rub the rim of a Mason jar with a lime wedge, and dip it into the lime zest mixture.
5. Pour the margarita into the salt-rimmed Mason jar, and garnish it with a watermelon wedge and mint sprig.

MAKE IT AHEAD: You can make the watermelon-cucumber juice up to a day in advance, and store it in the refrigerator in an airtight container. Just be sure to shake well before using.

BACKYARD MOVIE NIGHT

Most of the time I need no real reason at all to celebrate! Taking the time to entertain the ones you love without a specific occasion can make an event-free weekend something special.

I had been itching to put together an outdoor movie night for my friends and their kids. My parents had just renovated a beautiful historic home in downtown Franklin, Tennessee, that boasts an adorable courtyard and wraparound porch just begging to host a party.

Hang a white sheet, rent a projector, and invite everyone out for a movie night under the stars—the perfect treat in the midst of what can sometimes seem like an endless summer.

GET THE LOOK

For centerpieces I wanted to showcase summer's splendor, so I kept it simple, using flowers and greenery straight from the yard. Large, loose arrangements were held in vintage popcorn and peanut tins, keeping with the movie theme and creating a relaxed Southern-chic vibe. I used antique blue Ball jars to line the walk to the courtyard, which was filled with blankets and pillows so guests could spread out and make themselves comfortable. Vintage crates flipped upside down served as mini tables in the grass.

MOVIE TIME

Choosing the right movie is a must. Showcase an old classic like *Splendor in the Grass*, *To Kill a Mockingbird*, or *A Streetcar Named Desire* if your guests are all adults, or make it a family-friendly night with *The Sandlot* or *Chitty Chitty Bang Bang*. Even better? Keep it Southern with flicks such as *Steel Magnolias*, *Fried Green Tomatoes*, or *Driving Miss Daisy*.

THE MENU

Sure, the movie is the main attraction, but food is a close second. Re-create the excitement of the snack bar with a homemade popcorn stand. Fill glass jars with homemade popcorn creations such as rosemary Parmesan and salted caramel. Provide metal scoops for self-serving and berry containers for guests to take their selections back to their seats. I made oversized soft pretzels that everyone loved, served with an assortment of gourmet dipping sauces (think spicy mustard, brown sugar caramel, and beer cheese).

Fill a wagon with movie candy, peanuts, and old-fashioned sodas served over ice to make a mobile concession stand that can be pulled around to guests during the movie.

My favorite summer cocktail is simple yet chic: chilled sparking white wine with fruit Popsicles used as swizzle sticks. A sugary, icy Popsicle is the perfect summery addition to the bubbles of a good sparkling wine.

ENJOY THE PARTY!

A little extra preparation will help make your guests comfortable. Set out bug spray, have sweaters and blankets on hand in case the temperature drops, and tell friends to park away from the projector screen so headlights won't interrupt the film if someone must leave early.

MOVIE NIGHT POPCORN

ROSEMARY PARMESAN POPCORN

1/2 cup popcorn kernels, popped

5 tablespoons extra-virgin olive oil

3 tablespoons grated Parmigiano-Reggiano

1 tablespoon fresh rosemary, finely chopped

1/2 teaspoon fine sea salt

Makes 10 to 15 servings

1. Pour the popped popcorn into a large serving bowl.
2. In a separate bowl whisk together the olive oil, cheese, rosemary, and sea salt.
3. Pour the olive oil mixture over the popcorn, and toss well to coat the popcorn.

SALTED CARAMEL POPCORN

1/2 cup popcorn kernels, popped

1 cup (2 sticks) salted butter

1 cup light brown sugar

1/3 cup light corn syrup

11/2 to 2 teaspoons kosher or sea salt, divided

Makes 10 to 15 servings

1. Preheat the oven to 300 degrees. Line a large rimmed baking sheet with parchment paper.
2. Pour the popped popcorn into a large serving bowl. In a small saucepan melt together the butter, brown sugar, corn syrup, and 1 teaspoon of the salt over medium heat. Bring the mixture to a boil. Boil for 4 minutes without stirring.
3. Pour the caramel mixture over the popcorn, and toss the popcorn to coat it evenly. Pour the popcorn into the lined pan, sprinkle the remaining salt on top (1/2 to 1 teaspoon, depending on your personal taste preference), and place the pan in the oven. Bake for 30 minutes, stirring every 10 minutes.
4. Allow the popcorn to cool on a parchment paper–lined counter.

MAKE IT AHEAD: The Rosemary Parmesan Popcorn needs to be made the day of the event (as the popcorn will become greasy), but the Salted Caramel Popcorn can be made up to three days in advance and stored in an airtight container.

HOSTESS BASKETS

When people go out of their way to feed and entertain you, show your gratitude with a little something for the host or hostess.

A bottle of wine is always a welcome offering, but a unique gift basket is a present your hosts won't soon forget. From small and homemade to more extravagant, gift baskets can be tailored to fit any budget.

Start by selecting a theme. Think about whom you're gifting the basket to, the theme of the event, and how much you'd like to spend. Next, choosing a "basket" for your gift is just as important as its contents. Think outside the box (literally) when deciding on the container, and select something that becomes part of the gift. Finally, filling the basket should be fun and thoughtful. I love showcasing local products and including items that are on the top of my favorite-things list.

1. TEA FOR ONE

Fill a small picnic basket with items for a beautiful tea party for one. A teapot filled with fresh flowers, a vintage teacup and spoon, tea cookies, lemon curd, jam, honey, and a personalized calligraphy tag will make for a lovely and relaxing afternoon for your hostess the day after the party.

2. BARBECUE WITH THE BOYS

I love this lantern chock-full of chic barbecue favorites. A canteen, Turkish-T towel, soda, candle, and s'mores kit make for a fun evening with the guys.

3. BREAKFAST IN BED

After a long evening of cleaning dishes, your hostess will appreciate breakfast in bed the following morning. A basket full of coffee, pancakes and syrup, fresh-squeezed orange juice, fruit, muffins, and champagne for mimosas should do the trick!

MILKSHAKE SOCIAL

After a long, hot summer of pool parties, backyard fun, and playdates around the neighborhood, I thought we'd celebrate the end of the sunny season by inviting our neighbors over for a milkshake social. Forget about having a swimsuit-ready body! Elaborate milkshakes piled high with sweet treats take center stage, and a DIY milkshake bar encourages guests to create their own masterpieces.

As a kid, many nights after dinner my brother and I would sit on the counter and help my dad make chocolate milkshakes in a milkshake machine very similar to the one I used for this party: a metal cup, when pressed just perfectly against a lever, sets off a motor making a long metal paddle spin. A blender will get the job done, but a vintage milkshake machine like this one evokes that throwback goodness of a soda shop.

GET THE LOOK

When it comes to a party like this, bring on the color! Tall, extravagant milkshakes displayed on vintage jade cake stands were the focal point, set along the back of a bright-pink papier-mâché flamingo. A black-and-white polka dot backdrop set the stage, while black stools topped with flamingo fabric encouraged guests to take a seat and stay awhile.

THE MENU

Imagining the endless milkshake flavor combinations was so much fun for me. S'mores, chocolate, peanut butter, strawberry, chocolate-hazelnut, chocolate chip cookies, brownies, cupcakes, sprinkles, bananas, cotton candy, and whipped cream mixed with sweet ice cream—the options are limitless! I created several indulgent milkshakes for everyone to share and to spark guests' inspiration. Then I lined a window ledge with Mason jars of ingredients for guests to create their own.

Furthering the soda shop appeal, I served tiny burgers on square plates, shoestring fries in geometric aqua tumblers, and cotton candy milkshakes in tall, gold-striped glasses.

MAKE IT AHEAD

Prep milkshake ingredients in jars days in advance, then set them out for guests to make their own milkshakes.

ENJOY THE PARTY!

An entertaining trick I use quite often is getting my guests to participate in the creation of the food. Getting company involved encourages conversation and commingling, not to mention takes a good amount of effort off your plate!

MILKSHAKES

① S'MORES MILKSHAKE

1 (10-ounce) bag large marshmallows, divided

1/2 cup whole milk

1 teaspoon pure vanilla extract

2 cups (1 pint) good vanilla ice cream

Optional assorted toppings: whipped cream, toasted marshmallows chocolate, graham cracker crumbs, chocolate syrup

Makes 1 oversized milkshake

1. Chill the milkshake glass by placing it in the freezer.
2. Heat the broiler. Line a rimmed baking sheet with foil and coat it lightly with nonstick spray. Spread the marshmallows on the prepared baking sheet. Broil until the marshmallows begin to char (1 to 2 minutes). Let them cool completely. Once the marshmallows have cooled, put 2 or 3 marshmallows aside to use as topping.
3. Transfer the remaining broiled marshmallows into a blender, and add the milk. Blend until the ingredients are well mixed. Pause the blender to add the vanilla and ice cream to the marshmallow mixture, and blend until the milkshake is thick and smooth.
4. Pour the milkshake into the chilled glass, and finish with a dollop of fresh whipped cream, toasted marshmallows, and assorted toppings.

② STRAWBERRY SWEET TOOTH MILKSHAKE

1/2 pound frozen strawberries

3/4 cup whole milk

2 cups (1 pint) good strawberry ice cream

1 teaspoon pure vanilla extract

Optional assorted toppings: whipped cream, fresh strawberries, strawberry wafers, white chocolate syrup, sprinkles, cupcakes, macarons

Makes 1 oversized milkshake

1. Chill the milkshake glass by placing it in the freezer.
2. Place the frozen strawberries and milk in a blender, and blend until the strawberries are pulverized and smooth. Pause the blender to add the ice cream and vanilla, and blend until the milkshake is thick and smooth.
3. Pour the milkshake into the chilled glass, then finish with a dollop of fresh whipped cream, strawberries, and assorted toppings.

③ CHOCOLATE CHIP COOKIE MILKSHAKE

COOKIE DOUGH

1/2 cup unsalted butter (1 stick), softened

3/4 cup light brown sugar

1 teaspoon pure vanilla extract

1 cup all-purpose flour

1/2 teaspoon salt

1/4 cup milk

3/4 cup mini chocolate chips

MILKSHAKE

1 cup cookie dough, plus extra to line the glass

3/4 cup whole milk

2 cups (1 pint) good vanilla ice cream

Optional assorted toppings: whipped cream, cookie dough, chocolate chip cookies, mini chocolate chips

Makes 1 oversized milkshake

1. To make the cookie dough, in the bowl of an electric mixer fitted with the paddle attachment, beat the butter on high speed until creamy, about 1 minute. Switch the mixer to medium speed, and add the brown sugar. Beat until the butter and brown sugar are combined, scraping down the sides and bottom of the bowl as needed. On low speed add the vanilla, flour, and salt. Beat until all the ingredients are well mixed. The dough will be thick and heavy. Add the milk and beat on low for 30 seconds until it is incorporated. Then switch to high and beat for at least 2 minutes until the mixture is creamy. Gently fold in the chocolate chips. Set the dough aside at room temperature until you are ready to use it.
2. Line the rim of a glass with cookie dough, and place the glass in the freezer so the dough will harden.
3. To make the milkshake, in a blender combine the milk, ice cream, and 1 cup of the cookie dough, and blend until the milkshake is thick and smooth. Pour into the chilled glass, then finish with a dollop of fresh whipped cream and assorted toppings.

> **MAKE IT AHEAD:** Prepare the cookie dough up to three days in advance, and store it in the refrigerator in an airtight container. Bring it to room temperature before using.

④ PEANUT BUTTER PRETZEL MILKSHAKE

3/4 cup whole milk

1 teaspoon pure vanilla extract

1/4 cup chocolate syrup

2 tablespoons creamy peanut butter

2 cups (1 pint) good vanilla (or chocolate) ice cream

Optional assorted toppings: whipped cream, peanut butter, pretzels, peanut butter cookies, peanut butter cups, warm chocolate-hazelnut spread

Makes 1 oversized milkshake

1. Chill the milkshake glass by placing it in the freezer.
2. In a blender combine the milk, vanilla, chocolate syrup, peanut butter, and ice cream, and blend until the milkshake is thick and smooth.
3. Pour into the chilled glass, then finish with a dollop of fresh whipped cream and assorted toppings.

SUMMER MENU

When summer hits, it's hard to beat the fresh flavors of the earth. Seasonal vegetables abound, fresh seafood is readily available, and simple dishes are on the docket.

A couple summers ago we planted a little vegetable garden in a raised bed in our backyard with the hopes of simply keeping it alive. I wanted to teach my daughter where food comes from, encourage her to eat more vegetables, and simply enjoy some quality family time working together to create something special. My husband and I were shocked when it exploded with tomatoes, lettuce, okra, and herbs. The only problem we had was keeping Emmaline from eating all the tomatoes straight from the vine, red *and* green. She gobbled up hundreds of tomatoes that summer (no exaggeration), and we made the best memories tending to that little pile of dirt.

During the summer months, whatever we don't harvest from our own garden comes from the farmers' market: peaches, watermelon, squash, cucumbers, peppers, and corn—all inspiring and shaping unfussy, effortless meals perfect for entertaining.

- Strawberry Scones

- Homemade Cherry Limeade

- Rosé Granita

- Peach Caprese Salad

- Walnut and Lime Basil Pesto

- Fish Tacos with Grilled Corn Slaw and Strawberry Mango Salsa

- Blackberry Cobbler with Homemade Vanilla Ice Cream

- Banana Pudding with Salted Caramel

- Strawberry Shortcake

- Key Lime Coconut Bars

- Jacobs' Birthday Cake

STRAWBERRY SCONES

One summer morning when my counter was overflowing with fresh strawberries, I created this light strawberry scone recipe highlighting flavors of fresh lemon, almond extract, and Greek yogurt. You can freeze the dough and bake just a couple each morning for yourself or make them into mini versions for a crowd.

1 large egg

¼ cup plain Greek yogurt

½ cup milk

⅛ teaspoon almond extract

½ teaspoon pure vanilla extract

Zest from 1 lemon

2¼ cups all-purpose flour

½ cup sugar, plus more for sprinkling

1 tablespoon baking powder

½ teaspoon salt

8 tablespoons cold, unsalted butter, cut into small pieces

1 cup diced fresh strawberries

4 tablespoons butter, melted

Makes 8 large scones or 16 mini scones

1. Preheat the oven to 425 degrees. Line a baking sheet with a baking mat or parchment paper.
2. In a small bowl whisk together the egg, yogurt, milk, almond extract, vanilla, and lemon zest until blended.
3. In the bowl of a food processor combine the flour, sugar, baking powder, and salt. Pulse briefly to blend. Add the butter pieces to the bowl with the flour mixture, and pulse several times to cut the butter into the flour until the largest butter pieces are the size of small peas. Transfer the mixture to a large bowl.
4. Add the strawberries to the flour mixture, and toss to coat. Add the egg mixture, and gently fold together the ingredients with a fork or spatula until a sticky dough forms. Knead just a few times to ensure that the flour mixture is incorporated and the dough is cohesive.
5. Transfer the dough to a well-floured work surface, and pat it into a disc about 7 to 8 inches in diameter. The dough will be sticky—work more flour into the dough with your hands if needed until it's manageable. Slice the disc into 8 wedges (for smaller scones, slice each of those wedges in half).
6. Place the shaped scones on the prepared baking sheet, brush them with melted butter, and then sprinkle them with sugar. Bake the scones until they are lightly browned on top, about 15 to 20 minutes. Let them cool a few minutes before serving. Serve within a couple hours of baking (scones will easily become soggy because of the fresh fruit).

MAKE IT AHEAD: To freeze, transfer the unbaked shaped scones to a baking sheet, and place the pan in the freezer to chill the scones until firm, about 30 to 60 minutes. Wrap the scones individually, and store them in a freezer-safe bag until you are ready to bake them. Bake the scones as indicated above, adding a few minutes to the baking time until the crust is golden and crisp.

HOMEMADE CHERRY LIMEADE

I started making homemade cherry limeade for our annual Fourth of July party, and now it's become a special summer treat that I find myself making quite often. There's something about it that is quintessentially summer, and it's a childhood favorite that adults don't have to be ashamed to say they adore. Plus, it's great spiked with vodka for a cool cocktail.

1 (2-liter) bottle lemon-lime soda

1 cup freshly squeezed lime juice (about 8 to 10 limes)

1/2 cup grenadine

Nugget ice

Maraschino cherries and lime slices for garnish

Makes 8 servings

1. Combine the lemon-lime soda, lime juice, and grenadine in a large pitcher, and stir. Chill.
2. Pour into individual glasses filled with ice, garnishing each with cherries and limes.

MAKE IT AHEAD: You don't want to make this too far in advance or the soda will go flat, but you can make it just before guests arrive and store it in the refrigerator.

ROSÉ GRANITA

In the summer heat everyone craves frozen treats to help cool off. A strawberry champagne slushie? Yes, please! This could be the coolest treat ever created. Not only is it light, refreshing, and totally chic, but it's also great to make well in advance. Wow your guests by serving this as dessert in coupe or martini glasses topped with fresh mint.

1½ pounds strawberries, hulled and quartered, divided

1½ cups sugar

⅓ cup water

1 (750-milliliter) bottle chilled rosé champagne

2 tablespoons freshly squeezed lemon juice

Makes 12 servings

1. In a medium saucepan combine half of the strawberries with the sugar and ⅓ cup of water, and bring to a simmer. Cook over medium heat, stirring occasionally until the sugar is dissolved and the liquid is slightly thickened, about 5 minutes.
2. Transfer the strawberry mixture to a food processor. Add the remaining strawberries, and puree until smooth.
3. Strain the puree through a fine-mesh sieve set over a large bowl. Add the champagne and lemon juice, and mix well. Pour the mixture into a 9 x 13-inch glass or stainless steel baking pan.
4. Freeze the granita for 2 hours. Scrape the frozen edges into the center. Freeze for another 3 hours, scraping hourly, until the granita is icy and flaky. Freeze for 8 hours or overnight.
5. Scrape the granita into bowls and serve.

MAKE IT AHEAD: This granita can be made up to a week in advance and kept in the freezer. Simply scrape edges into the center, if needed, to regain the flaky consistency just before transferring to serving glasses.

PEACH CAPRESE SALAD

I know summer has officially arrived when The Peach Truck, a Nashville staple, is parked across the street from our house with a truckload of Georgia's finest. Without fail, each week we grab a bag of peaches and blow through them within days, fighting over the last one in the bottom of the bag.

I created this salad to take to a potluck. The Italian staple is taken to a whole new level by the simple addition of sweet summer peaches.

4 whole ripe tomatoes, sliced thick

4 whole ripe peaches, sliced thick

12 ounces fresh mozzarella cheese, sliced thick

Fresh basil leaves

Olive oil for drizzling

Balsamic vinegar for drizzling

Kosher salt and freshly ground black pepper

Makes 8 to 10 servings

1. Arrange the tomato, peach, and mozzarella slices on a platter, placing basil leaves between the layers.
2. Drizzle olive oil over the top of the salad, and then drizzle balsamic vinegar over the salad, getting a little bit on each slice. End with a sprinkling of kosher salt and black pepper.
3. Keep the salad at room temperature (for up to an hour) until you are ready to serve it.

WALNUT AND LIME BASIL PESTO

My go-to staple in summer is fresh pesto. I always have an abundance of basil in the garden and make this pesto on a weekly basis to keep in the fridge. It's great for impromptu dinner parties and quick summer suppers. Serve it on poached halibut, grilled salmon, and chicken, in pasta and pizza recipes, or simply with crackers as an appetizer.

1/4 cup walnuts

1 1/2 tablespoons chopped garlic (4 cloves)

2 1/2 cups fresh basil leaves, packed

1/2 teaspoon kosher salt

1/2 teaspoon freshly ground black pepper

1/4 cup of freshly squeezed lime juice (about 2 to 3 limes)

1/2 cups good olive oil

1/2 cup freshly grated Parmesan

Makes 1 cup

1. Place the walnuts and garlic in the bowl of a food processor fitted with a steel blade. Process for 15 seconds.
2. Add the basil, salt, and pepper.
3. With the processor running, slowly pour the lime juice and olive oil into the bowl through the feed tube, and process until the pesto is thoroughly pureed.
4. Add the Parmesan, and puree until you reach the desired consistency, about 20 seconds.
5. Use the pesto right away or store it in the refrigerator or freezer with a thin film of olive oil on top so the basil doesn't brown.

MAKE IT AHEAD: Store the pesto in the refrigerator in an airtight container, and drizzle the top with oil to prevent browning. Freeze the pesto in ice cube trays, and then store the frozen pesto cubes in plastic freezer bags in the freezer for up to six months.

FISH TACOS WITH GRILLED CORN SLAW AND STRAWBERRY MANGO SALSA

Though Nashville is definitely landlocked, we do have several good distributors who provide fresh seafood. These fish tacos are a local restaurant favorite that I re-created at home. This is one of my more involved recipes with lots of different components, but it's worth it! You can also prepare the corn slaw, salsa, and sauces in advance.

GRILLED CORN SLAW

4 ears fresh corn, kernels cut from the cob

1½ cups cabbage slaw mix (shredded red cabbage, white cabbage, carrots)

Juice of 1 lime

¼ cup white wine vinegar

Salt and freshly ground black pepper

½ cup queso fresco, crumbled

Handful fresh cilantro leaves, roughly chopped

Heat a grill pan over medium heat. Grill the corn on the hot grill pan, turning periodically until the corn is cooked and seared with grill marks. In a large bowl toss the cabbage mix with the lime juice and vinegar. Season with salt and pepper to taste. Once the corn has cooled, cut the kernels off the cob and add it to the bowl with the cabbage. Add the crumbled queso fresco and chopped cilantro, and stir to combine.

STRAWBERRY MANGO SALSA

½ cup diced strawberries

½ cup diced mango

1 jalapeño pepper, seeded and minced

2 tablespoons diced red onion

2 tablespoons chopped fresh cilantro

2 teaspoons honey or to taste

Juice of 1 lime

In a bowl toss together the strawberries, mango, jalapeño, onion, cilantro, honey (to taste), and lime juice. Serve immediately, or seal tightly and refrigerate until ready to use.

CILANTRO MOJO SAUCE

3 to 4 garlic cloves

1 bunch fresh cilantro

¼ teaspoon ground cumin

¾ teaspoon coarse salt

½ cup olive oil

4 to 5 tablespoons water

White wine vinegar to taste

Peel the garlic cloves. Trim the stems from the cilantro bunch. Process the garlic, cilantro, cumin, and salt in a food processor or blender to create a paste. While blending, drizzle in olive oil gradually. Add small amounts of water until the sauce is thick, but not as thick as a paste. Add 1 to 2 teaspoons of vinegar or more, according to your taste. Seal tightly and refrigerate.

CHIPOTLE CREMA

1/4 cup Greek yogurt

1 tablespoon adobo sauce from container of chipotle chile peppers

1 teaspoon freshly squeezed lime juice

1/2 teaspoon honey

Salt

In a bowl whisk together the Greek yogurt, adobo sauce, lime juice, and honey. Season with salt, and store it in the refrigerator in an airtight container.

FISH TACOS

2 tablespoons olive oil

Juice of 1 lime

1 tablespoon chili powder

1 jalapeño pepper, seeded and coarsely chopped

1/4 cup fresh cilantro, coarsely chopped, plus extra for garnish

1 pound flaky white fish (cod, tilapia, mahi mahi)

1 cup panko bread crumbs

Pinch of salt and freshly ground black pepper

8 whole wheat tortillas

Avocado, sliced

Makes 4 to 6 servings

Preheat the oven to 425 degrees. Place a cooling rack on a large baking sheet, and spray with cooking spray. In a small bowl whisk together the oil, lime juice, chili powder, jalapeño, and cilantro. Slice the fish into thin strips, and place it in the marinade. Let the fish sit for 15 minutes. Season the panko bread crumbs with salt and pepper. Dip each piece of fish in the bread crumbs, and lay them on a cooling rack over a baking sheet. Bake the fish for 10 to 15 minutes until it is cooked through.

Wrap the tortillas in a damp paper towel, and place them in the microwave for 30 seconds. Top each tortilla with 3 or 4 strips of warm fish. Drizzle the fish with Cilantro Mojo Sauce. Top the fish with Grilled Corn Slaw, fresh sliced avocado, Strawberry Mango Salsa, a dollop of Chipotle Crema, and chopped cilantro.

MAKE IT AHEAD: Make everything but the fish up to a day in advance. Bake the fish just before serving, and let guests assemble their own tacos.

BLACKBERRY COBBLER WITH HOMEMADE VANILLA ICE CREAM

When I was young, the long gravel road leading to my family's lake house was shaded by the most beautiful tree alley lined with moss, wild ferns, and loads of prickly blackberry bushes. We would spend hours picking blackberries with my grandfather, whom we called "Honey," then return to the house with full baskets and turn on the loud cranking ice cream maker on the porch. Nowadays, we pick blackberries from the fields on my in-laws' farm, and I can't help but miss Honey every time I make this blackberry cobbler and hear the crank of an old-fashioned ice cream maker.

1 pound fresh blackberries

3/4 cup sugar (more or less depending on sweetness of berries)

1/4 cup cornstarch

Zest and juice of 1 lemon

1 teaspoon pure vanilla extract

1 1/4 cups all-purpose flour

1/4 cup sugar

1 1/4 teaspoon baking powder

1/4 teaspoon baking soda

1/3 teaspoon salt

6 tablespoons (3/4 stick) unsalted butter, cut into small cubes and chilled

1/4 cup heavy cream

Makes 8 servings

1. Preheat the oven to 350 degrees.
2. Combine the blackberries, sugar, cornstarch, lemon zest and juice, and vanilla in a medium bowl. Pour the mixture into a greased 9-inch baking dish.
3. To make the dough, whisk together the flour, sugar, baking powder, baking soda, and salt. Use your fingertips to rub the butter into the flour mixture until it is the texture of coarse meal. Make a well in the center of the mixture. Pour the heavy cream into the well and stir it with a fork until the mixture comes together. Crumble the dough evenly over the top of the blackberry mixture.
4. Bake the cobbler for 40 minutes until the filling begins to bubble around the edges and the topping is golden brown. Let the cobbler cool for 10 minutes, and serve it with homemade vanilla ice cream.

HOMEMADE VANILLA ICE CREAM

3 cups whole milk

1 3/4 cups sugar

1/2 teaspoon salt

2 cups half-and-half

1 tablespoon pure vanilla extract

3 cups heavy cream

Makes 1 gallon

1. To make the ice cream, in a saucepan over a medium-high heat, scald the milk until bubbles form around the edges of the pan. Remove the pan from the heat.
2. Add the sugar and salt, and stir until dissolved. Stir in the half-and-half, vanilla, and heavy cream. Allow the mixture to cool completely.
3. Pour the mixture into a large bowl, cover it, and refrigerate it for at least an hour (overnight is best). Freeze per your ice cream machine's instructions.

MAKE IT AHEAD: This ice cream can be made up to one month in advance if it is packed and stored properly in the freezer. However, I like to cook the base the day before a party (making sure it has time to chill in the refrigerator to let the flavors meld) and then turn on the ice cream maker just before guests arrive. Licking the dasher is always a huge hit as everyone dives in for a taste. Plus, I think the texture is softer and creamier when the ice cream is fresh.

BANANA PUDDING WITH SALTED CARAMEL SAUCE

Banana pudding is a *serious* Southern staple. Every barbecue joint and meat-and-three restaurant has a variation of the dessert. There's a lot of dispute as to what is the "correct" way to make it. Warm or cold? Vanilla or banana pudding? Layered or stacked wafers? This recipe calls for very ripe bananas assembled with cold vanilla pudding and topped with caramel (in lieu of meringue). Single-serving Mason jars make for an adorable presentation. Serve it immediately so the wafers are still crisp, or let it rest a day in the refrigerator so everything melds together.

1 (14-ounce) can sweetened condensed milk

1½ cups ice cold water

1 (3.4-ounce) box instant vanilla pudding mix

3 cups heavy cream

1 box vanilla wafers

4 sliced bananas (very ripe)

Almond toffee for garnish (optional)

SALTED CARAMEL SAUCE

1 cup sugar

¼ cup water

¾ cup heavy cream

3½ tablespoons unsalted butter

1 teaspoon gray sea salt, crushed or kosher salt

Makes 8 half-pint (8-ounce) Mason jars

1. In the bowl of an electric mixer fitted with the paddle attachment, beat the sweetened condensed milk and water for about a minute. Add the pudding mix, and beat for about 2 more minutes. Transfer to a smaller bowl, cover, and refrigerate for at least 4 hours or overnight until firm.

2. In the bowl of an electric mixer fitted with the whisk attachment, whip the heavy cream on medium speed until stiff peaks form. With the mixer on low, add in the chilled pudding mixture until just combined and no streaks of pudding are visible.

3. In Mason jars layer the wafers, bananas, and pudding until you have 2 or 3 layers in each jar, ending with pudding. Cover each jar tightly with plastic wrap, and refrigerate the pudding for at least 30 minutes before serving or overnight.

4. To make the salted caramel sauce, in a heavy-bottomed saucepan combine the sugar and water over medium-low heat until the sugar dissolves. Increase the heat and bring to a boil, without stirring, swirling the pan if necessary. Boil until the syrup is a deep amber color, about 5 to 6 minutes. Remove the pan from the heat and carefully whisk in the heavy cream. The mixture will bubble. Stir in the butter and salt. Transfer the caramel to a dish and let it cool. Just before serving, drizzle each banana pudding Mason jar with salted caramel sauce, and garnish with toffee pieces.

MAKE IT AHEAD: Store the caramel sauce in the refrigerator for up to two weeks, and warm it before serving. Make the banana pudding up to a day in advance.

STRAWBERRY SHORTCAKE

My mom collaborated on a cookbook for the Monroe Carell Children's Hospital at Vanderbilt University in 2005. During that year, our dinner table was filled with recipes she was testing for the book. I think everyone agrees that this strawberry shortcake was the star of that book, and it ultimately became a family favorite. I guess the apple doesn't fall far from the tree!

2 cups all-purpose flour

1 cup white sugar

1 teaspoon baking powder

1/2 teaspoon salt

1/2 cup (1 stick) cold butter

2 large eggs

1 cup cold heavy cream

1/4 cup powdered sugar

1/2 teaspoon pure vanilla extract

4 cups strawberries sliced 1/4-inch thick (about 1 quart)

Fresh mint and blueberries for garnish

Makes 8 to 10 servings

1. Preheat the oven to 350 degrees. Butter and flour an 8-inch round cake pan.
2. Sift the flour, white sugar, baking powder, and salt into a bowl. Using a pastry cutter or your fingers, cut in the butter until the mixture is crumbly. Add the eggs and stir until the ingredients are just combined. Turn the dough out onto a lightly floured surface. Knead gently several times to form a ball. Press the dough evenly into the prepared pan. Bake for 30 to 35 minutes until lightly brown. Let the shortcake cool completely.
3. To make the whipped cream, in the bowl of an electric mixer fitted with the whisk attachment beat the cold cream with the powdered sugar and vanilla on medium-high speed until soft peaks form, being careful not to overbeat, as it will get to the consistency of butter, which is too thick.
4. Using a serrated knife, carefully slice the shortcake horizontally into two even layers. Top the first layer with half the whipped cream and strawberries. Place the second layer of shortcake on top, and top with the remaining whipped cream and strawberries. Garnish with mint (and blueberries for the 4th of July), if desired.

MAKE IT AHEAD: Make the shortcake up to a day in advance, and store it in an airtight container at room temperature. Make the whipped cream just before serving, then assemble the shortcake.

KEY LIME COCONUT BARS

Key lime pie is my favorite dessert. Tart and creamy, cool and refreshing, it's the perfect hot-summer-day confection. These bars feature a shortbread-like crust chock-full of crunchy coconut topped with a smooth, creamy key lime custard—summer's perfect pie made into a no-fork-needed bar.

1 cup shredded sweetened coconut, plus more for garnish

1½ cups all-purpose flour

½ cup powdered sugar

10 tablespoons cold unsalted butter, cut in small pieces

Egg yolks from 6 large eggs

2 (14-ounce) cans sweetened condensed milk

4 teaspoons grated key lime or regular lime zest, plus more for garnish

1 cup key lime juice (about 2 pounds of key limes)

Makes 24 bars

1. Preheat the oven to 350 degrees.
2. Spread the coconut on a rimmed baking sheet, and toast it until it is golden brown, about 6 to 8 minutes, tossing every 2 minutes to ensure even browning. Remove the pan from the oven, and transfer the coconut to a plate to cool.
3. In a large bowl combine the flour, sugar, and 1 cup toasted coconut. Using a pastry cutter or your fingers, cut the butter into the flour mixture until it resembles coarse meal. Press the mixture into a 9 x 13-inch pan, and bake until the crust is golden, about 15 to 20 minutes. Allow it to cool slightly.
4. Meanwhile, in a large bowl beat together the egg yolks and condensed milk with a whisk until thick. Gradually beat in the lime zest and juice.
5. Pour the egg and milk mixture into the cooled crust, and bake the bars until they are just hot, about 6 to 8 minutes.
6. Let the bars cool completely, then chill them until you are ready to serve (at least 3 hours).
7. Cut into bars and serve chilled. Before serving, sprinkle with toasted coconut and garnish with lime zest, if desired.

MAKE IT AHEAD: Make these bars the day before serving, and store them in the refrigerator in an airtight container.

JACOBS' BIRTHDAY CAKE

My husband, Brent, whom I call "Jacobs," has a summer birthday. He likes simple, straightforward food, and his yearly birthday cake—white cake with chocolate buttercream icing—is just that: special but completely fuss-free.

1 cup (2 sticks) butter, softened

1/2 cup vegetable shortening

2 cups sugar

5 large eggs, room temperature

3 cups all-purpose flour

2 teaspoons baking powder

1/4 teaspoon salt

1/2 cup whole milk, room temperature

1/2 cup buttermilk, room temperature

2 teaspoons pure vanilla extract

CHOCOLATE BUTTERCREAM

12 ounces semisweet chocolate, plus more for garnish

2 cups (4 sticks) unsalted butter, softened

3 tablespoons milk

1 1/2 teaspoon pure vanilla extract

3 cups sifted powdered sugar

Makes 1 cake, approximately 10 to 12 servings

> **MAKE IT AHEAD:**
> Make the cake the day before serving, and store it in an airtight container at room temperature. Make the buttercream and assemble the cake the day of the event.

1. Preheat the oven to 350 degrees. Butter and flour three 9-inch round cake pans.
2. In the bowl of an electric mixer fitted with the paddle attachment cream together the butter and shortening until light and fluffy. Slowly add the sugar 1 cup at a time, making sure to fully incorporate the first cup before adding the second. With the mixer on low speed, add the eggs, one at a time, scraping down the bowl after each addition.
3. In a separate bowl sift together the flour, baking powder, and salt. Pour the milk, buttermilk, and vanilla into a large measuring cup, and whisk together. In three parts, alternately add the flour mixture and the milk mixture to the batter, beginning and ending with the flour mixture. Mix until just combined.
4. Divide the batter among the pans. Bake, rotating the pans halfway through, until golden brown and a cake tester inserted in the center comes out clean, about 25 to 35 minutes. Transfer the pans to a wire rack. Once cooled, invert the cakes onto the racks, then reinvert, top side up. Cool completely.
5. To make the icing, place the chocolate into a microwave-safe bowl. Microwave on high for 30-second intervals, stirring after each until the chocolate is melted. Allow it to cool 3 to 5 minutes or until lukewarm.
6. In a large bowl beat the butter using an electric mixer fitted with the paddle attachment on medium speed for about 3 minutes or until creamy. Add the milk carefully, and beat until smooth. Add the melted chocolate, and beat well for 2 minutes. Add the vanilla, and beat for 3 minutes. Gradually add in the powdered sugar, and beat on low speed until creamy and of desired consistency.
7. To assemble the cake, slice the cakes in half horizontally to make four layers and ice with the icing. Shave some chocolate on top with a vegetable peeler.

Fall

FALL IS MY FAVORITE SEASON OF THEM ALL. BLUE JEANS, BOOTS, FOOTBALL, RED WINE, AND CHARCUTERIE PLATTERS EXPLODING WITH MEAT AND CHEESE—WHAT'S NOT TO LOVE?

The season of crisp air and falling leaves invites long drives in the country and picnicking the old-fashioned way. Pack a basket full of savory and sweet snacks, a blanket, and a wonderfully warming cider.

My family's favorite autumn activity is our annual trip to Gentry's Farm, in Franklin, Tennessee, for a hayride through the cow fields followed by pumpkin picking and lots of laughter on the tire swing that hangs from the oak tree beside the old barn. The cooler weather makes for an inviting picnic lunch, and we can never leave without a quick visit to feed the chickens.

We load up the car—with way too many orange Cinderella pumpkins—and head to my parents' house for Sunday-night supper around the bonfire, where we inevitably carve pumpkins and roast s'mores as the harvest moon rises.

AUTUMN TAILGATE

Now that the heat of late summer has given way to brisk autumn afternoons, we relish the notion of spending the entire day outside. It's time for tailgating—that rowdy, fun, pregame party awash in fan gear, delicious eats, and a beverage (or two). It is the quintessential American tradition that everyone can cheer for, no matter your team.

Brent and I still live in the town where we grew up. We love going to our alma mater's football games on chilly Friday nights to cheer on the Eagles. A Southern high school football game invokes feelings of nostalgia for idyllic, small-town America. Grabbing a pregame bite with old friends provides an opportunity for catching up and reminiscing about two-a-day football practices and cheerleading pep rallies.

Fall tailgating complete with autumnal flavors and rustic touches ushers in a season of community fellowship and football fun.

GET THE LOOK

Pack mood makers: vintage (or vintage-inspired) tartan thermoses, team pennants, plaid blankets, and even a hibachi grill to capture the palette of the season. Plaid blankets can serve as warm bleacher capes later during the game.

Eating outdoors requires dishware strong enough to hold in laps but lightweight enough to cart around. Vintage enamelware does the trick while still emphasizing the retro aesthetic. Wooden and metal serving trays are easy to pack, and Mason or Weck jars are durable and sealable, making them great for food storage or used as glassware. Remember mood lighting and take along lanterns for after the sun sets, and pack everything in picnic baskets for easy tote-ability.

THE MENU

The great autumn tradition of tailgating would be little without food and is much more fun with a deviation from the standard fare. Forget burgers and hot dogs; tailgating becomes très chic when you provide a more sophisticated spread. Plan to serve a fuss-free portable meal you can prepare ahead, full of fresh, seasonal produce and rich autumnal flavors.

Baguette sandwiches are not only delicious, but when wrapped in paper, they are portable and utensil free. Think of combinations like ham with blackberry jam, Camembert cheese and arugula, or steak with pesto, red onion, and plum tomatoes. Corn salad, fruit (clementines, grapes, and apples), and nuts make for light, healthy sides. Wow guests by serving cornbread baked right into Mason jars and topped with chili. Paper cones hold a homemade snack mix made of pretzels, mini marshmallows, cheese crackers, popcorn, and peanut butter M&M's.

Dress up copper mugs of warm spice tea with cinnamon sticks (and optional whiskey). Have red and white wine available along with craft beer in team koozies, and provide glass-bottled Cokes for kids.

Finally, never forget dessert—mini cherry hand pies are not only adorable but delicious, and Goo Goo Clusters (a Nashville favorite) are great to pack in pockets for a midgame treat.

ENJOY THE PARTY!

One great thing about tailgating is that everything is made ahead—unless you're grilling, which becomes part of the fun. Consider a few important tips when packing a meal to go. First, when planning your menu, choose items that won't spoil easily, avoiding foods with mayonnaise or dairy. Pack food in resealable containers to prevent spilling, and don't forget the necessities like plates, napkins, cups, ice, a blanket, and a bottle opener. Make cleanup easy by packing a trash bag and wet wipes.

MAKE IT AHEAD

When planning a tailgate menu, make sure you choose items that store and travel well.

it's fall y'all

HOT SPICE TEA

This hot tea is perfect to keep everyone warm on a chilly game day. Feel free to spike it with whiskey, and save the recipe for the holidays, as it makes the perfect Christmas tea.

5 quarts of water, divided

6 tea bags (I like using a cinnamon spice or chai)

1 cup sugar

2 cinnamon sticks

2 tablespoons mulling spices

Juice of 3 lemons

1 cup pineapple juice

1 cup orange juice

Makes 1½ gallons

1. Bring 1 quart of the water to a boil.
2. Turn off the heat, add in the tea bags, cover, and let steep per package requirements (about 3 to 5 minutes). Remove the tea bags, and add the remaining 4 quarts of water.
3. Turn the heat to high, and add the sugar, cinnamon sticks, and mulling spices. Bring to a boil for about 5 minutes until the sugar dissolves and the spices begin to become fragrant.
4. Reduce to a simmer, and remove the spices with a handheld fine-mesh strainer.
5. Add the lemon juice, pineapple juice, and orange juice, stirring until combined.
6. Remove from heat and serve immediately, or cool completely and store in the refrigerator for up to 1 week.

MAKE IT AHEAD: This tea is actually better made ahead of time, as the flavors further meld in the refrigerator. Make it up to a week in advance, and serve it warm from a thermos or percolator.

CHERRY HAND PIES

There's nothing cuter than a tiny pie. These hand pies are perfect for grab-and-go tailgating—no plates or utensils needed.

4 cups fresh or frozen sweet cherries

1¼ cups water

1 cup sugar

¼ cup cornstarch

2 tablespoons butter

¼ teaspoon salt

1 teaspoon almond extract

½ teaspoon pure vanilla extract

Pastry pie dough (recipe on pages 116–117)

1 large egg beaten with 1 tablespoon water for egg wash

Makes 1 dozen hand pies

1. Preheat the oven to 375 degrees. Line a rimmed baking sheet with a baking mat or parchment paper.
2. Combine the cherries with the water, sugar, and cornstarch in a saucepan over medium heat, stirring occasionally until thickened. Add the butter and salt.
3. Remove from the heat. Add the almond extract and vanilla. Let the mixture cool until room temperature (about 30 minutes).
4. Roll the pastry dough on a floured surface, and cut the desired shapes with 3-inch cookie cutter. Place the bottom pastry piece on the prepared baking sheet. Add 1 tablespoon pie filling. Cover with the top pastry, and crimp the edges together.
5. Brush the tops of the pastry with the egg wash, and make a small slit in each for ventilation.
6. Bake for 15 minutes. Let the hand pies cool completely before removing from the pan.

MAKE IT AHEAD: These hand pies can be made a day in advance and stored in an airtight container at room temperature.

WINE-TASTING PARTY

Whether you are a wine novice or an aficionado, a wine-tasting party is an elegant and fun way to entertain. Plus, comparing and discussing vino with your friends at a tasting is an easy way to learn about wine.

This past fall we invited a small group of friends over for a relaxed wine tasting. I kept the decor understated, using wooden and white accents, fresh herbs and produce in lieu of flowers, and paper table coverings, which made cleanup easy and red-wine stains a nonissue.

When it comes to choosing wine for a tasting like this, now's the time to deviate from your go-to bottles. Introduce guests to wine regions they may not be familiar with and select a diverse variety of flavors. Provide guests a list of what they'll be tasting with room for notes that they can take home.

Let guests graze on basic but filling dinner-worthy fare such as cheese, prosciutto, crostini, focaccia with dipping oils, fruit, and a little something *dolce* like these homemade orange ricotta donuts served with do-it-yourself affogato al caffè.

ORANGE RICOTTA DONUTS

Canola oil for frying

1 cup all-purpose flour

1/4 cup powdered sugar, plus more
for dusting

2 teaspoons baking powder

1/4 teaspoon salt

1 cup ricotta cheese

2 large eggs, beaten

1/2 cup whole milk

2 teaspoons grated orange zest

Raspberry sauce, store-bought

Chocolate sauce, store-bought

Makes 10 to 12 donuts

1. In a large heavy saucepan, add enough oil to reach the depth of 1¹/₂ inches. Heat the oil over medium-high heat until it registers 350 degrees on a deep-fry thermometer.
2. Meanwhile, in a medium bowl whisk together the flour, powdered sugar, baking powder, and salt. In a separate large bowl whisk together the ricotta, eggs, milk, and orange zest to blend, then whisk in the flour mixture until the batter just comes together.
3. Working in batches, using a 1¹/₄-ounce cookie scoop, fill the scoop with batter and lower the scoop into the hot oil, releasing the batter while the scoop is submerged in oil to achieve a circular shape. Fry the fritters, turning occasionally, for 3 to 4 minutes until they are deep golden brown and no longer doughy in the center. Using a slotted spoon, transfer the fritters to paper towels to drain. Return the oil to 350 degrees before cooking each batch.
4. Dust the donuts with powdered sugar, and serve warm with raspberry sauce and chocolate sauce for dipping.

PIE PARTY

No matter how you slice it, an old-fashioned pie party is a simple way to gather friends and family to savor the sumptuous holiday season. Pie is not only a staple of the Thanksgiving table, but it is a beloved year-round favorite. So why not make a party out of it?

Just think—a farm table in the middle of the woods covered in all different kinds of pies, wine, cider, and rustic decor surrounded by your favorite friends. Are you are starting to picture the wonderfulness a pie party can bring?

Host a pie party in your backyard, light a bonfire, and carve pumpkins. Or invite friends over to watch the big game, and delight everyone with a buffet of pies. Surprise your family with a pie party after Thanksgiving lunch, or treat your coworkers to a pie party in lieu of that awkward office holiday party. There are so many options to hosting this party . . . and, well, who doesn't love pie?

THE MENU

Sweet potato, pecan, fudge, apple, pumpkin—nothing sparks debate like the question of which holiday pie is best. The conclusion? Let's just say that I've never met a pie I didn't like!

Don't feel intimidated by the need to bake numerous pies. Invite friends and family to bake (or purchase and bring) their favorite pies. You'll end up with a magnificent assortment of sweet and savory and maybe even a few new recipes. Likewise, think beyond the traditional pie and make hand pies, fried pies, mini pies, or pie pops. Make tags to label the different pie flavors, and be sure to have to-go containers on hand to send leftovers home with guests.

I also served warm apple cider and chose wine that paired well with sweets. Both kept guests warm as the afternoon turned into a chilly evening.

MAKE IT AHEAD

Homemade piecrust can be made weeks in advance and frozen (pages 116–117).

GET THE LOOK

I wanted this outdoor event to be rustic chic, so I decorated with candles displayed in mercury glass and incorporated natural elements like pinecones, acorns, cotton branches, cranberries, and pomegranates (all easily accessible and affordable). We lit a fire pit close by to warm hands and used wooden rounds to display candles and pies at varying heights to create a layered look.

When creating a party like this, your serving pieces should reflect the rustic charm of your theme. Use pieces that have silver, pewter, and copper accents. I decided to keep the decor white with just a touch of red. Whatever color scheme you choose, make sure that it will complement the natural colors of the pies—the stars of your party.

ENJOY THE PARTY!

This is the perfect event to encourage guests' interaction by making it a potluck. You can invite everyone to bring something, have the party catered, or make all the pies yourself. Pies are easy to make ahead, and almost all are just as good served the day after they come out of the oven.

FUDGE PIE

BRÛLÉE-TOPPED PUMPKIN PIE

This twist on the traditional Thanksgiving pumpkin pie is a welcome update to an old favorite. Brûléeing the top adds a crunchy, sweet texture to the smooth pumpkin filling.

1 (16-ounce) can pumpkin puree (not pumpkin pie filling)

1 (14-ounce) can sweetened condensed milk

2 large eggs

1 tablespoon pure vanilla extract

½ teaspoon pumpkin pie spice

½ teaspoon ground cinnamon

¼ teaspoon ground ginger

½ cup packed light brown sugar

1 piecrust, blind-baked (recipe on page 116 and instructions on page 117)

Fine sugar for brûlée top

4 tablespoons superfine sugar, divided

Makes 1 pie, approximately 10 servings

1. Preheat the oven to 425 degrees.
2. Whisk the pumpkin puree, condensed milk, eggs, vanilla, pumpkin pie spice, cinnamon, ginger, and brown sugar together in a large bowl until the mixture is very smooth. Pour it into the blind-baked piecrust.
3. Bake for 15 minutes, then reduce the oven temperature to 350 degrees and bake for 40 minutes longer. Lightly cover the perimeter of the crust with foil if it starts to brown.
4. Remove the pie from the oven when the center is set, and let it cool completely. Refrigerate the pie until you are ready to serve it.
5. Just before serving, sprinkle the pie evenly with some of the superfine sugar. Heat the sugar with a butane torch until caramelized, turning the pie for even browning, about 1 minute. Let the pie stand until the topping hardens. To get a thick, caramelized sugar crust, repeat this, with just a light sprinkling each time. Return to the refrigerator until the topping hardens, about 30 minutes. Serve or keep refrigerated no more than 2 hours longer.

Note: If you don't have a butane torch, you can brûlée the top of the pie in your oven's broiler. Turn on broiler and lightly cover the perimeter of the pie's crust to prevent browning. Sprinkle pie evenly with 2 tablespoons fine sugar and place under broiler until top is caramelized. Watch closely to prevent burning. Remove the pie from the oven, and let it stand until the topping hardens. To get a thick, caramelized sugar crust, repeat this, with just a light sprinkling each time. Return the pie to the refrigerator.

MAKE IT AHEAD: Make the pie the day before, and keep it in the refrigerator. About 30 minutes before serving, brûlée the top and return the pie to the refrigerator to set.

BLACKBERRY PIE

Summer brings an abundance of blackberries that inevitably end up in gallon bags in my freezer. I came up with this blackberry pie recipe as a fall alternative to summer's blackberry cobbler.

---

3 cups of blackberries (fresh or frozen)

1¼ cups sugar (more or less, depending on the sweetness of your blackberries)

1½ cups water

¼ cup cornstarch

1 tablespoon lemon juice

2 tablespoons butter

Pinch of salt

Dash of nutmeg

Pastry pie dough (recipe on pages 116–117)

Makes 1 pie, approximately 10 servings

1. Preheat the oven to 400 degrees.
2. In a saucepan over medium heat, cook the blackberries, sugar, water, and cornstarch until thick, stirring occasionally. Add the lemon juice, butter, salt, and nutmeg, and stir until the butter is melted and incorporated. Remove the pan from the heat and let the mixture cool to room temperature.
3. To prepare the crust, divide the chilled pie dough in half (one half for the bottom crust, one half for the top crust). Return the unused half to the refrigerator. Roll out the dough for the bottom on a lightly floured surface to ¼-inch thickness and 12-inch diameter crust if you are using a 9-inch pie pan. Line the bottom of your pie pan with the dough, leaving any overhanging dough. Chill the in refrigerator while you roll out the top crust.
4. For the top crust, roll out the remaining chilled dough on a lightly floured surface to ¼-inch thickness and about a 12-inch diameter. To create lattice work, using a sharp knife or pizza cutter, cut the dough into long even strips, ½-inch to ¾-inch wide, depending on how thick you want your lattice strips.
5. Pour the cooled blackberry pie filling into the bottom crust.
6. Create a lattice design using the cut dough strips for the top.
7. Place the pie on a baking sheet (to catch any spillage during baking) and bake at 400 degrees for 10 minutes. Reduce the heat to 350 and bake for 30 minutes. If needed, place a sheet of aluminum foil over the pie (or use a pie protector) to protect the edges and top from burning. Allow the pie to cool to room temperature before serving.

MAKE IT AHEAD: Make the pie a day in advance, and store it at room temperature until you are ready to serve it.

HOW TO MAKE THE PERFECT PIECRUST

A good pie is all about the crust. Sure, lard and shortening produce a tender, flaky crust, but they can't compete with the flavor of butter. The key to making a perfectly flaky butter crust is to keep all ingredients and working materials cold—the colder the fat when you put the pie into the oven, the greater the chance for flakiness.

2/3 cup warm water

2 tablespoons sugar

1 teaspoon salt

1 pound (4 sticks) cold unsalted butter, cut into 1/2-inch cubes (bigger pieces will make your dough puffy)

4 1/2 cups all-purpose flour, plus more for rolling

Makes 2 piecrusts

1. In a small bowl of warm water, dissolve the sugar and salt. Place the butter in the bowl of an electric mixer. Measure out the flour into a separate large bowl. Place the bowl of flour, the butter in the electric mixer bowl, and the mixer paddle in the freezer. Place the sugar mixture in the refrigerator. Let everything cool for at least 30 minutes (do not leave the butter in the freezer for more than 30 minutes, as you don't want it to freeze solid).
2. In the chilled bowl of an electric mixer fitted with a paddle attachment, combine the cold butter and flour. With your fingertips (not the palms of your hand, as they are too warm), toss the butter in the flour until each cube is lightly coated. Squeeze the butter between your fingertips to create thin discs. Do not overwork—you want everything to stay cold.
3. Return the bowl to the electric mixture and with the chilled paddle beat the flour-butter mixture on low speed to just break up the butter, about 30 seconds. Add the sugar mixture all at once, and raise the speed to medium-low. Beat just until the dough comes together in big chunks, then immediately turn off the mixer.
4. Divide the chunks of dough in half, and very gently pat each chunk into a round 1-inch-thick disc (this will make it easier to roll out). Wrap each tightly in plastic wrap and refrigerate until firm, about 1 hour, before rolling, or place the wrapped dough in a sealed freezer bag and place in the freezer for up to 3 months.

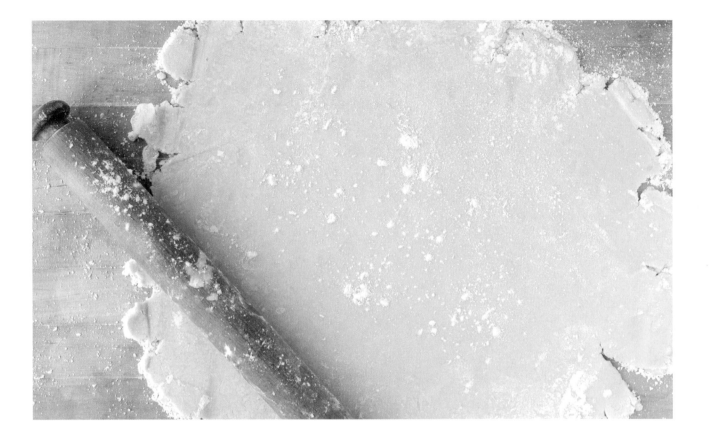

5. When you are ready to use the pie dough, let it thaw for 24 hours in the refrigerator, if frozen. Place the dough on a lightly floured surface. Hit the dough several times with rolling pin to slightly soften. Start rolling out the dough, working from the center out, and stop rolling before you reach the edge (being careful that everything is the same thickness). Roll the dough until you reach $1/8$-inch thickness.

6. Lightly grease the pie plate with nonstick spray before putting in the dough (this will make taking the slices out of the pan much easier later). Place the dough in a pie dish, and trim and crimp the edges of the dough. Wrap the pie pan in plastic and place it back in the freezer for another hour (this will help keep your crust from getting soggy from the filling).

Note: If a recipe calls for blind-baking the crust, preheat the oven to 425 degrees. Line the pie dough, already spread in the pie dish, with wax paper and fill the pan with pie weights. Bake the crust for 20 minutes, then remove it from the oven and take out the pie weights and the wax paper liner. Lower the oven temperature to 375 degrees. Return the pie to the oven to bake for an additional 15 minutes until the crust is golden. Remove the piecrust from the oven and let it cool completely before using.

MAKE IT AHEAD: You can refrigerate the dough discs for up to one day or freeze them for up to three months.

CAKE

HARVEST PICNIC

To celebrate the arrival of fall, I invited my friends to go with me to Bloomsbury Farm, located in Smyrna, Tennessee, for an afternoon of picking vegetables, noshing on fine food, and toasting a new season.

Upon arrival, we took a tour of the 400-acre farm with owner and farmer Lauren Palmer and learned how the crops are tended and harvested. We watched sweet potatoes being pulled out of the ground, helped weed the beds in the hoop house, and even tried our hand at picking broccoli and cauliflower in the fields. After our baskets were full, we found a shady spot overlooking a field of eggplants and bell peppers for a gourmet picnic.

After spending this glorious day at Bloomsbury Farm, I was ready to move in and become a farmer. I don't think they'll mind much . . . as long as I bring cake.

GET THE LOOK

Pumpkin planters filled with cabbage and burlap bags planted with herbs served as centerpieces for our al fresco lunch. Everyone sat on heirloom quilts and snacked on a charcuterie board filled with local meats and cheeses while I opened bottles of wine and Saison ale chilled in old enamel buckets.

THE MENU

I packed individual lunches in burlap sacks labeled with each guest's name and included a cloth napkin tied with a fork and a sprig of rosemary.

MAKE IT AHEAD

Package and label lunches for guests so you're not spending time serving everyone.

Lunch highlighted produce found at the farm—eggplant, prosciutto, and fresh basil pesto pressed sandwiches; roasted butternut squash and pumpkin seed quinoa salad; sweet potato and apple chips; sparkling apple cider; and dark chocolate–covered pretzels sprinkled with toffee.

We ended the afternoon with a cake that definitely stole the show: a three-layer apple coffee chocolate cake iced with peanut butter cream cheese icing; drizzled with dark chocolate and a bourbon salted caramel; and topped with peanuts, flaky sea salt, and caramel apples.

ENJOY THE PARTY!

When packing for a large-scale picnic like this, you don't have to use a traditional picnic basket. Any basket, tote bag, cooler, or even a wagon will do the trick. Pack food in resealable containers to prevent spilling (I like reusable Mason or Weck jars). Everything can be made ahead and stored in a cooler until time to eat.

ROASTED BUTTERNUT SQUASH QUINOA SALAD

Quinoa is such a great base for seasonal flavors—for simply mixing in whatever vegetables or ingredients are fresh or on hand. This squash version is ideal for a fall picnic because it not only highlights autumnal flavor, but is also easily stored in a cooler.

3 cups butternut squash, cut into ½-inch cubes

1 tablespoon olive oil

Salt and freshly ground black pepper

1 cup uncooked quinoa

⅓ cup dried cranberries

⅓ cup red onion, finely chopped

3 tablespoons toasted pumpkin seeds

BALSAMIC VINAIGRETTE

½ cup olive oil

¼ cup balsamic vinegar

1 teaspoon honey

1 teaspoon Dijon mustard

1 garlic clove, minced

Salt and freshly ground black pepper

Makes 6 to 8 servings

1. Preheat the oven to 400 degrees.
2. In a large bowl toss the butternut squash with the olive oil. Season with salt and pepper to taste. Arrange the squash on a rimmed baking sheet in a single layer. Roast for 20 to 25 minutes until the squash is tender and lightly browned.
3. While the squash is roasting, rinse the quinoa under cold water until the water runs clear, and then cook it per the package directions. Allow it to cool.
4. Remove the squash from the oven, and allow it to cool slightly.
5. Make the balsamic vinaigrette by whisking the olive oil, balsamic vinegar, honey, Dijon, and garlic in a small bowl until combined. Season with salt and pepper to taste.
6. To assemble the salad, combine the cooked quinoa, roasted squash, cranberries, red onion, and toasted pumpkin seeds in a large bowl. Add the vinaigrette, and mix until combined. Season with salt and pepper to taste. Chill the salad in the refrigerator until you are ready to serve it.

MAKE IT AHEAD: Make this salad up to a day in advance, and store it in the refrigerator in an airtight container.

HARVEST CARAMEL APPLE CHOCOLATE CAKE

Wow! This cake . . . Weeks before the planned day out at Bloomsbury Farm, Brent and I listed all our favorite fall dessert flavors: chocolate, peanut butter, caramel, apple, pumpkin, coffee, and bourbon. I got to work, playing with ingredient combinations, and this cake was born. You're welcome.

CAKE

2 cups all-purpose flour

2 cups granulated sugar

1 cup unsweetened cocoa powder

2 teaspoons baking soda

2 teaspoons baking powder

1 teaspoon ground cinnamon

1/2 teaspoon pumpkin pie spice

1 teaspoon salt

3 large eggs, room temperature

1 cup applesauce

1/2 cup canola oil

1 tablespoon pure vanilla extract

1 cup hot, strong brewed coffee

SALTED CARAMEL

2 cups sugar

1 cup honey

1/2 cup bourbon

1/2 cup apple cider

2 cups heavy cream

1/2 cup (1 stick) butter

1 tablespoon pure vanilla extract

1/2 teaspoon kosher salt

PEANUT BUTTER ICING

1 cup (2 sticks) unsalted butter, softened

4 ounces cream cheese, softened

2 cups powdered sugar

1/2 cup creamy peanut butter

1/3 cup salted caramel (cooled, recipe above)

2 teaspoons pure vanilla extract

1. To make the cake, preheat the oven to 350 degrees. Butter and flour three 8-inch round cake pans, lining each with parchment paper.
2. In a medium bowl whisk together the flour, sugar, cocoa powder, baking soda, baking powder, cinnamon, pumpkin pie spice, and salt until just combined.
3. In the bowl of an electric mixer fitted with a paddle attachment, beat together the eggs, applesauce, canola oil, and vanilla until smooth.
4. Slowly add the flour mixture to the egg mixture with the mixer on low until there are no clumps of flour. Add the hot coffee, and mix until just combined.
5. Pour the batter equally into the three cake pans and bake for 20 to 25 minutes until the cakes are set and a toothpick inserted into the center comes out clean. Let cool completely.
6. To make the salted caramel, place the sugar, honey, bourbon, and apple cider in a large saucepan over medium-high heat. Bring to a boil. Let the mixture boil, without stirring, for about 9 minutes until it is light golden in color. Add the heavy cream, butter, and vanilla, slowly stirring them into the pan. Boil for 10 to 15 minutes or until a candy thermometer reads 210 degrees, stirring frequently. Remove the sauce from the heat and add the kosher salt. Cover and store the caramel at room temperature until you are ready to pour it over the cake.
7. To make the icing, add the butter, cream cheese, and powdered sugar to the bowl of an electric mixer fitted with the whisk attachment. Beat them together until the butter is light and fluffy, about 4 minutes. Add the peanut butter, 1/3 cup of the cooled caramel, and vanilla, then beat, scraping down the sides as needed, another 2 minutes or until there are no streaks.
8. To assemble the cake, spread icing between the layers and over the top and sides of the cake. Place the cake in the refrigerator to set.

CHOCOLATE DRIZZLE

8 ounces bittersweet chocolate, chopped

1/2 cup heavy cream

GARNISHES

1/2 cup salted peanuts for garnish

Flaky salt for sprinkling

3 small apples

Twigs or wooden sticks for apple handles

Makes 1 three-layer round cake, approximately 12 servings

9. To make the chocolate drizzle, place the chocolate and cream in a microwave-safe bowl. Microwave on high for 30-second intervals, stirring after each interval until the chocolate is melted. Allow the sauce to cool for 3 to 5 minutes, and then pour the sauce onto the middle of the cake and spread it to just the sides, allowing the sauce to drip down the sides of the cake. Place the cake in the refrigerator, preferably overnight, but for at least an hour, making sure the chocolate is set and the icing is firm.

10. To make the caramel apple garnishes, place the pot of salted caramel back over medium-high heat and bring it to a boil. Boil for 15 to 20 minutes or until a candy thermometer reads between 220 and 230 degrees. Remove the sauce from the stove, and let it cool for 15 to 20 minutes, stirring every so often. Make sure the caramel does not become too stiff. If it hardens you will not be able to dip the apples. While the sauce cools, push the twigs or wooden sticks into the top of the apples. Line a baking sheet with wax paper.

11. When the caramel has cooled enough to touch, pour about half the caramel over the cake and allow it to fall down the sides of the cake. Working quickly, dip the apples into the remaining caramel and place them on the center of cake. Sprinkle the cake with flaky salt and peanuts.

12. Refrigerate the cake until the caramel is firm, at least 30 minutes. Once the caramel is firm, store the cake in the refrigerator until you are ready to serve it. Allow the cake to sit 30 minutes at room temperature before serving.

13. The recipe will make extra caramel. Store it in the refrigerator in an airtight container for up to two weeks.

S'MORES BAR

Some of my favorite things about being a kid were the campfires my family built on cool autumn evenings and getting to toast fluffy marshmallows on sticks found in the yard until their snow-white skins turned golden brown and their insides were gooey. We would sandwich them with chocolate bars between graham crackers and devour the fire-kissed treats, always asking for "s'more."

Turns out the likability of s'mores extends far beyond childhood. I've never met an adult who can resist the goodness of a warm marshmallow-chocolate-cookie sandwich.

At your next dinner party or barbecue, in lieu of a traditional dessert, surprise guests with a s'mores bar. Yes, make sure to have on hand the classic combination of marshmallows, milk chocolate, and graham crackers for the traditionalists, but for your more adventurous friends, put out ingredients encouraging creativity, like cookies, English chocolate biscuits, candy bars, caramel, chocolate-hazelnut spread, peanut butter, bananas, and peanut butter cups.

You'll need a campfire or grill and some sticks for roasting the marshmallows. Provide guests with containers (like these adorable berry boxes) to take their selections to the bonfire and use as to-go containers later in the evening. Your guests will swoon over their creations and will forever talk about that evening of ooey-gooey, sticky-hands, chocolate-on-your-face fun!

FALL MENU

All's right in the world when you've invited your favorite people to share a meal, the room's snug and cozy, and a family-style dinner is on the table. Guests settle in for a relaxed evening, and your only hope is that everyone lingers awhile.

Coming off the heat of summer, fall is a welcome friend. Life begins to slow again as kids get back into the routine of school and easy family weeknight dinners become necessary. Growing up, I always had athletic practices after school, and by the time I arrived home for dinner, I was ravenous. My poor mother! She always had a beautiful, warm homemade dinner prepared (broccoli cheese soup, chicken pot pie, pot roast, and poppy seed chicken were some of our favorites), and our family would sit down around the kitchen table and eat together.

Whether you're hosting a dinner party for friends or serving a simple weeknight supper for your kids, gathering around the table for a meal is an important for reconnecting with the ones you love. Fall is the perfect time for warm, heartier dishes that soothe the soul and encourage everyone to unwind around the table.

- Whole Wheat Flaxseed Pumpkin Waffles
- Brown Sugar Pecan Sourdough Sticky Buns
- Charcuterie Platter
- Popovers
- Mom's Yeast Rolls
- Smoked Brisket Chili
- Skillet Cheddar Dill Cornbread
- Pomegranate Thai Chicken Enchiladas
- Skillet Roasted Chicken Ratatouille
- Spiced Pecan Pumpkin Quick Bread
- Chocolate Chip Cookies
- Chocolate-Hazelnut Brownies with Pretzel Graham Cracker Crust
- Salted Oatmeal Cornflake Cookies

WHOLE WHEAT FLAXSEED PUMPKIN WAFFLES

I'm hard-pressed not to put pumpkin in *everything* this time of year. These pumpkin waffles are crunchy on the outside with a soft and seasonally spicy interior. Topped with tart Granny Smith apples and sweet maple syrup, breakfast just got a whole lot more exciting.

2 cups whole wheat flour

3 tablespoons brown sugar

2 teaspoons baking powder

1 teaspoon baking soda

1 1/2 teaspoon ground cinnamon

1/2 teaspoon ground ginger

1/2 teaspoon ground nutmeg

1/2 teaspoon salt

1 1/2 cups low-fat milk

1 cup pumpkin puree

2 large eggs

1 teaspoon pure vanilla extract

2 tablespoons ground flaxseed

Cubed Granny Smith apples, cinnamon, and maple syrup for garnish

Makes 6 waffles

1. Combine the flour, brown sugar, baking powder, baking soda, cinnamon, ginger, nutmeg, and salt in a medium bowl.
2. Place the milk, pumpkin puree, eggs, vanilla, and flaxseed into the container of a blender, and secure the lid. Start the blender at low speed and quickly increase the speed to high. Blend for 20 seconds. Reduce the speed to low and remove the lid plug. Add the flour mixture slowly through the lid plug opening, and blend for an additional 10 seconds until the flour incorporated. Let the batter sit at room temperature for 5 to 10 minutes before cooking.
3. Coat a waffle iron with cooking spray and preheat. For each waffle, spoon about $1/2$ cup of the batter onto the hot waffle iron, spreading the batter to the edges. Cook each waffle for 5 to 7 minutes until the steaming stops. Repeat the procedure with the remaining batter.
4. Garnish with cubed apples, cinnamon, and warm maple syrup.

MAKE IT AHEAD: Make this batter up to a day in advance, and store it in the refrigerator in an airtight container. You can also freeze cooked waffles by letting them cool completely and placing them in individual freezer bags in the freezer. To cook the frozen waffles, place in a toaster oven until warmed through.

BROWN SUGAR PECAN SOURDOUGH STICKY BUNS

My friend Valerie introduced me to making sourdough bread and provided me with a starter that literally lives in my refrigerator. I love using the dough to make other things like cinnamon rolls and these sticky buns. If you don't have a sourdough starter, you can substitute a basic sweet bread recipe or use store-bought refrigerated biscuits.

1 cup sourdough starter

2¹/2 cups warm water, divided

¼ cup potato flakes

³/4 cup sugar

¹/2 cup canola oil

1 tablespoon salt

5 cups bread flour

2 cups chopped pecans, toasted

1 cup (2 sticks) butter, softened

2 teaspoons pure vanilla extract

2 teaspoons maple flavoring

2 cups dark brown sugar

4 teaspoons ground cinnamon

Makes 2 dozen sticky buns

1. To feed the starter, stir together the starter, 1 cup of the warm water, potato flakes, and sugar in a nonmetal bowl. Cover lightly with cloth and let it sit for 8 to 12 hours at room temperature. After 8 to 12 hours, split the mixture into two parts and put one of these halves back in a jar and into the refrigerator.

2. To make the dough, use an electric mixer fitted with a dough hook to mix 1 cup of the starter, the remaining 1¹/2 cups of warm water, canola oil, salt, and bread flour until the dough is a workable consistency and starts to pull away from the sides of the bowl (add more or less flour as needed). Place the dough on a floured surface, and knead it until it is no longer sticky. Place the dough into a greased nonmetal bowl, and cover it lightly with a cloth. Let it sit in a warm place for 8 to 12 hours or until it doubles in size.

3. After the dough has risen, butter two 12-cup standard muffin tins and sprinkle enough chopped pecans into each cup to just cover each bottom.

4. To assemble the rolls, remove half of the dough from the bowl. On a floured baking surface, roll the dough thin into a large rectangle.

5. To make the filling, place the softened butter into a medium bowl. Using a rubber spatula, mix the vanilla and maple flavoring into the butter. Using an offset spatula, spread half of the butter mixture evenly over the surface of the dough. Mix the brown sugar and cinnamon together in a bowl. Generously sprinkle half of the brown sugar mixture over the top of the butter.

6. Beginning with the long side facing you, tightly roll the dough away from you into a log, then pinch the edge of the dough to seal. Cut the dough crosswise into 1¹/2-inch pieces until you have 12 sticky buns. Place each cross-sectional piece into the prepared muffin cups, spiral side down. Repeat the process with the remaining dough and fill the second muffin tin.

7. Lightly cover the tins with a kitchen towel, and place them in a warm place. Let them rise for 8 to 10 hours (or until the buns double in size).

8. Preheat the oven to 350 degrees. Place the muffin tins on baking sheets to catch any overflow. Bake until the tops are golden brown, about 25 to 30 minutes. Remove from the oven and let the buns cool slightly. Invert the muffin tins over a serving platter. Let the buns cool slightly before serving.

CHARCUTERIE PLATTER

I love giant platters of amazing cheeses with lots of goodies to go with them. There is something for everyone, and it's a great way to encourage guests to mingle and chat. The best part? Assembling a stunning fruit and cheese platter requires absolutely no cooking!

Cured meats, such as salami, prosciutto, and pancetta

Hard cheeses, such as aged Cheddar and Parmesan

Soft cheeses, such as Brie, Camembert, and goat cheese

Semisoft cheeses, such as Havarti and Gouda

Crusty bread slices

Crackers

Fruit, such as grapes, figs, pears, and apples

Nuts

Honey

Wine jelly

1. There are several key principles to follow to be sure your platter looks festive and is easy for guests to help themselves. The first, and most important, is to buy good-quality ingredients.

2. Start with a selection of natural deli meats, then add an interesting assortment of cheeses: hard sharp cheeses, soft creamy ones, and pungent blue cheeses. Look for an interesting mix of flavors, textures, and colors. Refrigerate them after buying, but bring them to room temperature a couple hours before serving.

3. Second, be sure to have a platter or wooden board that is flat and large enough to hold the cheeses without crowding them. Arrange the cheeses with the cut sides facing out and with several small cheese knives. Be sure to label everything as it encourages guests to try different kinds when they know what they're eating.

4. Third, to finish the platter, add sliced breads, crackers, and fruit. Common fruits for platters are grapes, figs, pears, and apples. Use what's in season, though. Mandarin and blood oranges are beautiful in the winter months, while berries add a colorful punch in the warmer seasons.

5. Overall, the simpler the design, the better the platter looks. Group each kind of cheese together, and add one large bunch of green or red grapes to create a visual focal point. Fill in the spaces with cured meats, bread slices, crackers, nuts, honey, and jelly.

MAKE IT AHEAD: Assemble your platter an hour or two before guests arrive. Cover and allow the meats and cheeses to come to room temperature.

POPOVERS

Meet my best friend: the popover. These delicious little puppies are a mainstay in my kitchen. This simple, magical combination of milk, eggs, and flour creates the most incredibly airy and crispy puffs you could ever imagine. Get creative by adding Gruyère and chives, cinnamon and sugar, or just keep it simple and enjoy the basic recipe. Either way, you'll agree that this is just the beginning of a lifelong friendship.

1½ tablespoons unsalted butter, melted (and cooled to room temperature), divided, plus softened butter for greasing pans

3 extra-large eggs, room temperature

1½ cups milk, room temperature

1½ cups all-purpose flour

¾ teaspoon kosher salt

Makes 6 popovers

1. Preheat the oven to 425 degrees.
2. Using a pastry brush, coat an aluminum popover pan or muffin tin with 1 tablespoon of the melted butter, and put the tin in the hot oven for 2 minutes.
3. Meanwhile, in a large bowl whisk together the eggs and milk until frothy (about a minute). Add the flour, salt, and the remaining ½ tablespoon of melted butter, and whisk until the batter is the consistency of heavy cream with some small lumps remaining. Remove the popover pan from the oven, and quickly fill each cup three-quarters full with batter. Bake for 30 minutes until the tops are golden brown. Do not open the oven during baking.
4. Popovers lose their crunch if they linger in the pan, so turn them out onto a wire rack and poke a small hole in the side of each with a paring knife to let the steam escape. Serve immediately.

For Gruyère and Chives Popovers: Add ½ cup of shredded Gruyère and 1 tablespoon of minced chives to the popover batter and bake per the directions.

For Cinnamon-Sugar Popovers: Bake per the directions and let popovers cool on a metal rack. In a small bowl combine ½ cup of sugar and 1½ teaspoons of cinnamon. Brush each popover with melted butter and then roll them in the cinnamon-sugar, coating each popover.

MOM'S YEAST ROLLS

These rolls are a Thanksgiving mainstay. You can't have Thanksgiving without yeast rolls, and this recipe is a foolproof family favorite. I like to make these rolls in advance, freeze them, and then bake just before dinner.

¼ cup lukewarm water (110 degrees)

1 envelope active dry yeast

2 large eggs

½ cup sugar

1 teaspoon salt

6 cups all-purpose flour, divided

1¼ cups water

½ cup vegetable oil

¼ cup (½ stick) butter, melted

Makes approximately 3 dozen rolls

1. Measure the lukewarm water in a measuring cup, and add the yeast. Stir until the yeast is completely dissolved. Let the mixture stand until the yeast begins to foam vigorously, about 5 to 10 minutes.

2. Add the yeast mixture to the bowl of an electric mixer fitted with the bread hook. Add the eggs, sugar, and salt, and mix until just combined. Add 2 cups of flour, and mix until well incorporated. Add the water and oil alternately with the remaining 4 cups of flour, mixing well after each addition, and beginning and ending with flour.

3. Roll the dough out on a well-floured surface (work more flour into the dough, if needed). Cut the dough with a 2-inch biscuit cutter. Dip each circle halfway into the butter, then fold each circle in half. Place the folded circles into greased 13-inch round pans. Cover lightly with a towel and let the rolls rise in a warm place for 2 to 3 hours or until doubled in size. Preheat the oven to 400 degrees and bake for 15 minutes until golden.

MAKE IT AHEAD: Bake the rolls until just before golden, remove them from the oven, and let them cool completely. Place the pans in freezer-safe bags, and freeze until the day of the event. Bake the frozen rolls at 400 degrees, covered in foil, for 15 minutes, then bake them uncovered for another 10 minutes.

SKILLET CHEDDAR DILL CORNBREAD

My cast-iron skillet is my most-used piece of cooking equipment. It gets superhot, is naturally nonstick, and is easy to clean. There are a couple keys to keeping your iron skillet in top working condition. Never let dish soap touch it (as it will suck out the moisture), simply rinse or wipe it out to clean, make sure it dries completely before storage, and oil it after each use. Take care of it, and it will take care of you!

---

3 cups all-purpose flour

1 cup yellow cornmeal

1/2 cup sugar

2 tablespoons baking powder

2 teaspoons kosher salt

2 cups buttermilk

3 extra-large eggs, lightly beaten

1/2 pound (2 sticks) unsalted butter, melted, plus extra to grease the pan

8 ounces grated extra-sharp Cheddar, about 2 cups

2 tablespoons minced fresh dill

2 tablespoons butter

2 tablespoons vegetable oil

Makes 10 to 12 servings

1. Preheat the oven to 350 degrees.
2. In a large bowl, combine the flour, cornmeal, sugar, baking powder, and salt with a whisk. In separate bowl, combine the buttermilk, eggs, and butter. With a wooden spoon, stir the wet ingredients into the dry until most of the lumps are dissolved, being careful not to overmix. Mix in the cheese and dill, and allow the mixture to sit at room temperature for 20 minutes.
3. Meanwhile, place the 2 tablespoons of butter and 2 tablespoons of vegetable oil in a 10-inch cast-iron skillet, and place the mixture in the preheated oven until it is hot and bubbly, about 5 minutes. Take the hot skillet out of the oven and carefully pour in the batter, smoothing the top, if needed.
4. Bake for 30 to 35 minutes until a toothpick comes out clean. Cool the cornbread and cut it into large wedges. Serve the cornbread warm or at room temperature.

SMOKED BRISKET CHILI

My stepdad, John, cooks our family's Sunday-night suppers. The grandkids play with the dogs on the porch or run around the pool while "Poppy" pulls something out of his smoker that's been cooking for days. In the fall and winter, he always has a big pot of something warm and comforting on the stove, like gumbo or chili, that he dishes out as we sit around the kitchen island. This recipe is my take on his smoked brisket chili, adding molasses, beer, and chocolate. Because that's how I roll.

2 tablespoons vegetable oil, divided

2 medium onions (about 2 cups), diced

3 small jalapeños, stems and seeds removed and discarded, and flesh cut into 1/2-inch pieces

1 green bell pepper, cut into 1/2-inch pieces

4 medium garlic cloves, minced

3 tablespoons cornmeal

2 teaspoons dried oregano

2 teaspoons ground cumin

2 teaspoons cocoa powder

1/4 teaspoon cayenne pepper (optional)

2 tablespoons chili powder

1 (28-ounce) can crushed tomatoes

2 teaspoons dark molasses

2 1/2 cups low-sodium chicken broth

1 (15-ounce) can pinto beans, drained and rinsed

1 (15-ounce) can kidney beans, drained and rinsed

1 (15-ounce) can black beans, drained and rinsed

2 pounds ground beef

Salt and pepper

1 (12-ounce) bottle mild-flavored lager

2 pounds cooked smoked brisket

Optional assorted toppings: sour cream, grated sharp Cheddar cheese, diced avocado, chopped red or green onion, chopped cilantro, lime wedges

Makes 8 to 10 servings

1. Preheat the oven to 300 degrees.
2. Heat 1 tablespoon of the oil in a large Dutch oven over medium-high heat. Add the onion, jalapeños, and green pepper. Cook, stirring occasionally, until the moisture has evaporated and the vegetables are softened, about 7 to 9 minutes. Add the garlic and cook until fragrant, about 1 minute. Add the cornmeal, oregano, cumin, cocoa powder, cayenne pepper, chili powder, tomatoes, and molasses, and stir until well combined. Add the chicken broth and beans, then reduce the heat to a simmer.
3. Meanwhile, heat the remaining 1 tablespoon of oil in a skillet over medium-high heat. Sprinkle the ground beef with salt and pepper, add to the skillet, and stir occasionally until the meat is cooked through and browned. Transfer the meat to the Dutch oven. Add the bottle of lager to the skillet, scraping the bottom of the pan to loosen any browned bits, and bring to a simmer. Transfer the lager to the Dutch oven. Add the smoked brisket to the Dutch oven, and stir to combine.
4. Cover the pot and transfer it to the oven. Allow the chili to cook for about 1 1/2 to 2 hours. Let the chili stand, uncovered, for 10 minutes. Stir it well and season to taste with salt before serving. Top with desired garnishes.

Note: If you don't want to smoke your own brisket, you can always buy it already cooked from your local barbecue restaurant.

MAKE IT AHEAD: Make the chili up to three days in advance. Let the chili cool completely, and store it in a covered Dutch oven in the refrigerator. When ready to serve, return the Dutch oven to the stove top and slowly heat the chili until hot, stirring often.

POMEGRANATE THAI CHICKEN ENCHILADAS

My cooking repertoire consists of Southern classics and family recipes. These enchiladas are a step outside my classic American recipe box. I enjoyed experimenting with ethnic flavors to create a warm, crowd-pleasing dish that is a pleasant departure from my more traditional go-tos. Serve with saffron rice, skinny margaritas (recipe on page 31), chips, and guacamole.

SAUCE

1½ cups sweet Thai chili sauce

½ cup soy sauce

⅓ cup dark brown sugar

1 tablespoon peanut butter

1 tablespoon tomato paste

¾ cup pomegranate juice

¼ cup rice vinegar

1 lime, juiced

1 teaspoon fish sauce

2 cloves garlic, minced or grated

2 tablespoons fresh ginger, grated

½ teaspoon crushed red pepper flakes

½ teaspoon freshly ground black pepper

ENCHILADAS

1 rotisserie chicken, meat removed and shredded (about 1 pound)

1 red bell pepper, sliced thin

1 orange bell pepper, sliced thin

½ cup cilantro, chopped

1½ cups mozzarella cheese, shredded, divided

8 to 10 flour tortillas

Diced avocado, pomegranate arils, chopped cilantro, green onions, and queso fresco for garnish

Makes 6 servings

1. Preheat the oven to 350 degrees. Spray a 9 x 13-inch baking dish with nonstick spray.

2. To make the sauce, in a medium sauce pan, whisk together the Thai chili sauce, soy sauce, brown sugar, peanut butter, tomato paste, pomegranate juice, rice vinegar, lime juice, fish sauce, garlic, ginger, crushed red pepper, and black pepper. Bring the sauce to a boil over medium-high heat, reduce the heat, and simmer for 10 to 15 minutes until sauce has thickened slightly. Remove the pan from the heat.

3. In the meantime, in a medium bowl add the shredded chicken, sliced bell peppers, cilantro, and 1 cup of the mozzarella. When the sauce has cooled slightly, pour in about ¾ cup, or just enough to coat the chicken. Toss well to coat.

4. To assemble the enchiladas, spoon a little of the chicken mixture down the center of each tortilla, tuck and roll the tortilla, then place the enchilada seam side down into the baking dish. Pour and spread the remainder of the sauce over the top of the enchiladas, and top with the remaining ½ cup of mozzarella.

5. Bake for 30 minutes until the cheese is melted. Remove the enchiladas from the oven and serve with diced avocado, pomegranate arils, cilantro, green onions, and queso fresco.

MAKE IT AHEAD: Assemble the enchiladas the day before (do not bake). Be sure the enchiladas are room temperature before you cover and refrigerate. When ready to serve, bake per the directions.

SKILLET ROASTED CHICKEN RATATOUILLE

When Emmaline was a newborn, I was desperate for a simple, hearty, healthy dish that could not only satisfy my family, but also friends coming over to meet her. Thus, this very simple one-pot wonder was born. It uses fresh ingredients and is best served with mashed potatoes and warm, crusty bread.

1/4 cup plus 1 tablespoon extra-virgin olive oil, plus more for rubbing

1 medium eggplant, cut into 1-inch cubes

1 medium zucchini, cut into 1-inch cubes

2 tablespoons minced garlic

2 cups cherry tomatoes

5 sprigs thyme

Coarse salt and freshly ground black pepper

2 large (or 4 small) bone-in, skin-on chicken breasts

Makes 2 to 4 servings

1. Preheat the oven to 450 degrees.
2. In a large cast-iron skillet, heat 1/4 cup of oil over medium-high heat. Add the eggplant and cook, stirring frequently until just beginning to brown, about 4 minutes. Add the zucchini, garlic, and the remaining 1 tablespoon of oil. Cook, stirring, until the garlic is fragrant, about 1 minute. Stir in the tomatoes and thyme, then season with salt and pepper.
3. Season the chicken on both sides with salt and pepper, and rub with oil. Add the chicken to the skillet on top of the vegetables, skin side up, and place the skillet in the oven. Roast until the chicken is cooked through, about 25 to 30 minutes. Turn oven to broil, and continue to cook until the chicken skin is golden brown and the juices are bubbly, 1 to 2 minutes longer. Let the ratatouille rest 10 minutes before serving.

SPICED PECAN PUMPKIN QUICK BREAD

A friend asked me to create a homemade recipe to match the expensive seasonal pumpkin bread mix that she and her family loved. I bought the mix and set out to create a cheaper (and healthier) version of the tried-and-true favorite. In the end, taste-testers (i.e., my husband) couldn't tell the difference between the store's mix and mine. Of course, I think the homemade version tastes better. It is soft, perfectly spiced with a robust pumpkin flavor, and made with love. Me: 1. Store-bought: 0.

3/4 cup pumpkin puree

2 large eggs

1/2 cup vegetable oil

1/2 cup buttermilk

1/2 cup white sugar

1 cup brown sugar

1 3/4 cups all-purpose flour

1 teaspoon baking soda

1/2 teaspoon salt

1/2 teaspoon ground cinnamon

1/2 teaspoon pumpkin pie spice

1/4 teaspoon ground ginger

1/4 teaspoon ground nutmeg

1/4 cup pecans, finely chopped

Makes 1 large loaf or 4 mini loaves

1. Preheat the oven to 350 degrees. Butter and flour a 9 1/2 x 4 1/2-inch loaf pan (or four mini loaf pans).
2. In a large bowl mix together the pumpkin puree, eggs, oil, buttermilk, white sugar, and brown sugar until well blended. In a separate bowl whisk together the flour, baking soda, salt, cinnamon, pumpkin pie spice, ginger, and nutmeg. Stir the flour mixture into the pumpkin mixture until just blended. Add the pecans and mix until just blended. Pour the batter into the prepared pan(s).
3. Bake for about 50 minutes in the preheated oven (if baking mini loaves, bake for about 25 minutes). Loaves are done when a toothpick inserted into the center comes out clean.

MAKE IT AHEAD: This bread can be made the day before, left to cool, and then stored in an airtight container. I like to make the mini loaves, place them in small cellophane bags, tie them with baker's twine, and deliver these as homemade gifts for teachers and neighbors.

CHOCOLATE CHIP COOKIES

Over the years I've baked hundreds—maybe thousands!—of chocolate chip cookies. I have been making them from scratch since my youth, and I'm always trying to improve my recipe. I firmly believe that chocolate chip cookies should be soft and chewy in the center, crisp on the edges, sweet with brown sugar, salty with a crunch, and perfectly speckled with just the right amount of chocolate. Years and years ago, they were the first recipe I shared on my blog, and they were the first recipe on my list for this book. This recipe makes giant cookies with big pools of melted chocolate, and each is dusted with flaky sea salt. The dough is chilled, allowing the flavors to meld, making these cookies taste like they are from the fanciest bakery in town.

1¼ cups (2½ sticks) unsalted butter, softened

1¼ cups light brown sugar

1 cup white sugar

2 large eggs

2 teaspoons pure vanilla extract

1¼ teaspoons baking soda

1½ teaspoons baking powder

1½ teaspoons kosher salt

3½ cups all-purpose flour

8 ounces semisweet chocolate baking discs

Flaky sea salt

Makes 16 large cookies

1. In the bowl of an electric mixer fitted with the paddle attachment, cream the butter, brown sugar, and white sugar together on medium speed until the mixture is light and fluffy, about 3 to 4 minutes. Add the eggs, one at a time, and mix to combine. Add the vanilla, mix, then scrape down the bowl. Add the baking soda, baking powder, and salt to the dough, and mix until fully combined. Add the flour all at once, and mix it in short bursts until just combined (do not overmix). Add the chocolate pieces and mix on low speed until just mixed in. Cover the bowl with plastic wrap, and chill in the fridge for a minimum of 24 hours and up to 3 days.

2. Preheat the oven to 350 degrees. Line two baking sheets with baking mats or parchment paper. Form the dough into 3½-ounce balls, a little larger than a golf ball. Arrange the dough balls very far apart on sheets (as the cookies will be up to 5 inches across once baked), and sprinkle the top of each with a few flecks of sea salt.

3. Bake the cookies for 12 to 17 minutes until they are golden all over. Allow the cookies to cool on the trays for 10 minutes, then transfer them to wire racks.

Tip: I have just recently started using semisweet chocolate baking discs in large cookies like these. You can certainly use chocolate chips, but the next time you are at a specialty grocery store, look for the baking discs. They melt beautifully, creating ribbons of chocolate through every bite.

MAKE IT AHEAD: Cookie dough can be made up to three days in advance and left to cool in the refrigerator. Cookies are best baked on the day of serving.

CHOCOLATE-HAZELNUT BROWNIES WITH PRETZEL GRAHAM CRACKER CRUST

I love snacking on pretzels dipped in Nutella. Sweet and salty—a dangerous combination. One afternoon while scraping the bottom of the Nutella jar with the very last pretzel (no judgment, please!), I had a thought . . . a brilliant thought: *Why not make Nutella brownies with a pretzel crust?* This rich three-ingredient Nutella brownie atop a crunchy, salty graham cracker crust is seriously good and ridiculously addicting. You've been warned.

CRUST

1 cup graham cracker crumbs

1 cup pretzel crumbs, plus more pretzels for decorating

1/2 cup sugar

3/4 cup (1 1/2 sticks) butter, melted

BROWNIES

2 1/2 cups chocolate-hazelnut spread, such as Nutella [this is approximately 1 (22 1/2-ounce) jar], reserve a little to drizzle on top

1 cup all-purpose flour

3 large eggs

Makes two dozen 2-inch brownies

1. Preheat the oven to 350 degrees. Line a 9 x 13-inch pan with parchment paper.
2. To make the crust, in a large bowl mix together the graham cracker crumbs, pretzel crumbs, sugar, and melted butter. Press into the bottom of the prepared pan, and bake for 6 to 7 minutes until set. Remove the pan from the oven and allow the crust to cool.
3. To make the brownies, in an electric mixer fitted with the paddle attachment mix together the chocolate-hazelnut spread, flour, and eggs until just combined. Pour this mixture over the cooled crust, and spread it to the edges. Bake until the surface looks set and slightly crisp, about 25 minutes. Let the brownies cool slightly, then remove them from the pan by lifting the parchment.
4. Let the brownies cool completely. Arrange the pretzels on top and drizzle with the remaining chocolate-hazelnut spread (place the jar in the microwave for approximately 20 seconds to make the spread easier to drizzle).
5. Slice the brownies into 2-inch squares and serve.

MAKE IT AHEAD: These brownies are good made the day before. Store them in an airtight container at room temperature.

SALTED OATMEAL CORNFLAKE COOKIES

When I attended the opening of trendy bakery Sprinkles' Nashville 12 South location, instead of ordering a box of cupcakes, like most people in line, I was drawn to the cookies on display in the pastry counter. Upon first bite, I knew the Salted Oatmeal Cornflake Cookie was my long-lost soul mate. I was blown away by its amazingness and immediately started to work on a copycat recipe. These cookies are soft and chewy, sweet and salty, and altogether wonderful.

1 cup (2 sticks) butter, softened

1 cup firmly packed light brown sugar

1/2 cup white sugar

2 large eggs

2 teaspoons pure vanilla extract

1 3/4 cups all-purpose flour

1 teaspoon baking soda

1/2 teaspoon salt

3 cups quick-cooking oats

2 heaping cups cornflakes

Sea salt

Makes 18 large cookies

MAKE IT AHEAD:
Cookie dough can be made a day in advance and left to chill in the refrigerator. Cookies are best baked the day of serving.

1. Preheat the oven to 325 degrees.
2. In the bowl of an electric mixer fitted with the paddle attachment, beat together the butter, brown sugar, and white sugar until light and fluffy. Beat in the eggs one at a time, then mix in the vanilla.
3. In a separate bowl whisk together the flour, baking soda, and salt. With the mixer on low, add the flour mixture to the creamed mixture until just blended. Mix in the oats until just incorporated. Remove the bowl from the mixer and add the cornflakes, gently folding to avoid crushing the cornflakes.
4. With a spoon, scoop out the dough and roll between the palms of your hands to create a walnut-size ball. Do not use a cookie scoop, as it will crush the cornflakes. Repeat until all the dough is rolled into balls. Place the dough balls on a baking sheet, and refrigerate the dough for at least 30 minutes.
5. Remove the dough from the refrigerator, and arrange the cookies on a baking sheet, leaving 2 inches between each cookie. Flatten each dough ball with your fingers or the bottom of a glass (reshaping the edges of the dough if needed to make a round cookie), and sprinkle the top of each cookie with sea salt.
6. Bake for 12 to 15 minutes in the preheated oven. Bake in multiple batches, if needed. Allow the cookies to cool on the baking sheet for 5 minutes before transferring them to a wire rack to cool completely.

Winter

THERE'S SOMETHING MAGICAL ABOUT THAT FIRST FROST OF WINTER.

When those first snow flurries fall, with them come enchanting feelings of childhood memories. 'Tis the season of ritual, as we look to re-create those emotions of holidays past.

Some of my favorite holiday memories center around my grandmother's dining room table. For Christmas Eve dinner, she would adorn her formal table with figurines of carolers, china embellished with Christmas trees, and red-stemmed water glasses. When I was little, she let me craft place cards with each family member's name, and occasionally she'd spring a game on us during dinner—asking us to say something we were thankful for or something we loved about the person next to us. Then we would move into the den, where my grandmother would linger in the doorway in her poinsettia apron while my grandfather read the Christmas story of baby Jesus and the youngest grandchild set up the nativity.

Now, as an adult with my own growing family, I cherish the customs and celebrations of my childhood but am intentional about creating new traditions of our own that will foster lasting memories for my children.

GINGERBREAD HOUSE DECORATING PARTY

Decorating a gingerbread house is a centuries-old holiday tradition. Sugary creations topped with delectable, colorful candies—what better way is there to celebrate the season? Gather friends and family together for a kid-friendly Christmas party that makes everyone's holiday a little sweeter.

GET THE LOOK

Let the kid-at-heart be your inspiration when planning your party decorations. Brightly colored gumdrops, candy canes, and gummies take center stage. Jars of marshmallows and vintage-inspired hard candies are easy centerpieces.

I topped a long farm table with a paper table runner and paper place mats. Child-friendly and easy to clean up, paper table coverings are totally on trend. These red-and-white-striped table runners and candy cane place mats were playful and geometrically chic.

A completed gingerbread house makes a perfect centerpiece for the table. Not only is it a great focal point, but it also serves as inspiration for party guests while they decorate their own houses. Guests were wowed by the gingerbread replica I made of Nashville's Draper James storefront. Make your own replica of your home, a city landmark, or a favorite childhood memory. I also decorated giant gingerbread men and gingerbread snowflakes, showcasing them in sugar-filled glass hurricanes to create snowy dioramas.

THE MENU

Everyone will undoubtedly have a blast eating candy while decorating their gingerbread houses, so keep the additional refreshments to a minimum. Hot chocolate is a crowd-pleaser for children and adults alike. I topped mugs with giant homemade marshmallows and peppermint sticks, and I constructed miniature gingerbread houses to perch on the rim of each mug. A tray of decorated sugar cookies and gingerbread men not only aligns with the theme, but the treats were also irresistible.

MAKE IT AHEAD

Gingerbread houses can be preassembled up to a week in advance.

ENJOY THE PARTY!

Construct the gingerbread houses for each child ahead of time so that all the kids have to do is have fun decorating. You can buy premade kits or bake and construct your own (pages 162–163).

I made the gingerbread house the centerpiece of each place setting and added a personalized name card and paper cups full of assorted candies. Each guest was given a pastry bag filled with icing to decorate with and to attach the candy to their holiday home. Younger children may need a little help with this part, so parents can ice while the kids attach the candy.

Have cake boxes on hand to send kids home with their finished gingerbread houses, and use favor bags to let everyone take home extra candy.

GINGERBREAD HOUSE

This gingerbread recipe is not meant to be eaten. It creates a hard, sturdy gingerbread perfect for constructing gingerbread houses. It makes enough dough for the two side walls, the front and the back walls, and the two roof sections. Plus, scraps can be rerolled to make roof tiles, trees, stars, and figures. Print out a template online, or create your own by cutting out cardstock sheets.

6³/4 cups all-purpose flour

4¹/2 teaspoons ground ginger

1¹/2 teaspoons ground cinnamon

1¹/2 teaspoons baking soda

1¹/2 teaspoons salt

1¹/2 cups solid vegetable shortening

1¹/2 cups dark brown sugar

3 large eggs

³/4 cup dark molasses

ROYAL ICING

Egg whites from 4 large eggs

7 to 7¹/2 cups powdered white sugar

Makes 1 (7 x 10-inch) gingerbread house

1. In a large bowl sift together the flour, ginger, cinnamon, baking soda, and salt.
2. In an electric mixer fitted with the paddle attachment, cream the shortening and brown sugar until fluffy. Beat in the eggs one at a time. Add the molasses, and beat on high speed until well blended. Add ¹/4 of the flour mixture at a time, beating at low speed until dough forms.
3. Divide the dough into six equal pieces, and wrap in plastic. Chill in the refrigerator for at least 6 hours.
4. Heat the oven to 350 degrees. On a well-floured surface, roll out the dough to ¹/8-inch thickness. Cut it into the desired shapes using a template. Place the dough shapes on ungreased baking sheets, and chill until firm, about 15 minutes. Bake for 15 minutes until the gingerbread is firm in the center but not dark around the edges.
5. To make the icing, in the bowl of an electric mixer fitted with the whisk attachment, beat the egg whites on medium-high speed until very foamy, about 1 minute. Add ¹/2 cup of the powdered sugar. Beat until well blended. Add the remaining cups of sugar, ¹/2 cup at a time, beating until each addition is well blended and scraping down the sides of the bowl as needed. Beat the icing at high speed until it is very thick and stiff, about 5 minutes. Transfer the icing to a piping bag, and use the icing immediately to assemble the walls.

MAKE IT AHEAD: Set aside a couple hours over three days to make this gingerbread house (one day to make the dough, one day to roll out and bake the gingerbread, and one day to assemble the house). This house can be made up to one month in advance.

HOT CHOCOLATE PARTY

A hot chocolate party is an event that both kids and adults can get on board with. Forget about the pressures of hosting a huge dinner, and invite your friends to a fun party they'll adore. We hosted this relaxed holiday open house at The Red House, an event space in downtown Franklin, Tennessee, where loved ones stopped by for a fun after-dinner treat.

I took inspiration from The Red House's vintage music poster collection and kept the color scheme simple by just using black and white with a punch of red. I loved the bright primary colors of the posters, and they gave the whole look of the party an edgy, throwback vibe.

We served an assortment of hot chocolate flavors so guests could create the perfect cozy drink. I made pitchers of white hot chocolate and milk hot chocolate for variety and offered decanters of cognac and Kahlúa for adults. Festive toppings and add-ins made each cup special and encouraged mingling as guests created their own concoctions. I made homemade marshmallows in the shape of snowflakes, and Nutella and peanut butter whipped cream to adorn mugs of cocoa. On a black paper table runner, I labeled different topping options, including peppermint sticks, shaved chocolate, caramel, Junior Mints, cinnamon sticks, and toffee.

Oreos stacked in the shape of a tiered cake was the perfect stunner for the black-and-white color scheme, and mid-party, I lit a sparkler on top and encouraged guests to dig in.

DECADENT HOT CHOCOLATE

Exceptional hot chocolate starts with the finest chocolate. The high-quality stuff is worth the splurge, as the chocolate's unique flavors will actually come through more with the addition of warm milk.

6 ounces semisweet chocolate, chopped into small pieces

1/3 cup unsweetened cocoa powder

6 cups whole milk, divided

1/2 teaspoon salt

3/4 cup sugar, or to taste

Marshmallows or whipped cream for garnish

Makes 6 servings

In a small saucepan mix the chocolate, cocoa powder, and 2 cups of the milk over low heat. Stir continuously until the chocolate is completely melted. Add the remaining 4 cups of milk and the salt. Stir, allowing it to heat the rest of the way through. Stir in sugar to taste, and continue to heat until it is completely dissolved. Pour the hot chocolate into mugs and top with marshmallows or whipped cream, if desired.

MAKE IT AHEAD: Make this hot chocolate recipe up to a day in advance. Allow it to cool completely, store it in the refrigerator in an airtight container, and reheat it when ready to serve.

Menu

STARTER
charcuterie board
SEASONAL MEAT AND CHEESE
WITH BRICK OVEN BREAD

SALAD
pomegranate apple salad
ARTISAN LETTUCE, POMEGRANATE, APPLE,
ROASTED BEETS, ORANGE, PECANS,
CREAMY CHEVRE, CITRUS VINAIGRETTE

ENTRÉE
short ribs
RED WINE BRAISED BEAR CREEK FARM BEEF,
CELERY ROOT PUREE,
OVEN CURRY SEASONED BEETS,
CELERY LEAF HERB SALAD

DESSERT
MALTED CARAMEL PECAN PIE

February 27th, 2016

WHISKEY TASTING

Whoever said whiskey is just for the boys never met a Southern girl. I gathered my girlfriends for a handsome girls' night featuring a Southern whiskey tasting dapper enough for the gentlemen but perfectly planned for the ladies.

Start the evening off with the whiskey tasting. Provide three to six whiskeys, and conduct the tasting before serving dinner, as the food can distort the taste. Start with lighter, milder whiskeys while your taste buds are still unaffected and can better detect the subtle aromas. Then proceed to stronger whiskeys, as their aroma often still lingers in the mouth long after the tasting and affects everything you try afterward.

Encourage guests to make notes during the tasting to remember their favorites, and always think ahead about providing your guests with a safe ride home (i.e., a rideshare service or designated driver).

ENJOY THE PARTY!

Forget an Evite and invite guests with formal invitations. Enlist the help of a designer to capture the feel of the party. Nashville-based design duo Tenn Hens Design created this invitation suite, presenting antlers and woodgrain with a feminine flair. The watercolor details and calligraphed personal touches were irresistible.

GET THE LOOK

Not everyone has a home fit to host a party—or they don't want the mess! You can still personalize an event at a restaurant by setting the table yourself. For this intimate dinner, I wanted the table to highlight the elegant rustic sensibility of the venue, feeling both chic and relaxed. Spode Woodland Hunting Dog dishes combined feminine florals with masculine hunting dog motifs, and wooden chargers and coasters added texture and paired perfectly with the gold-detailed flatware. I brought the outdoors in with a moss table runner flecked with river rocks and deer antlers. Barley twist and brass candlesticks holding long gray tapers made for an elegant, eclectic mix.

THE MENU

If you are hosting the party in a restaurant, have the bartender lead the way by helping to choose whiskeys for your tasting. If you are hosting at home, seek advice from your local liquor store owner.

Menus at each place setting highlighted a preselected dinner—a simple and elegant way to cut costs when hosting a restaurant event. Guests noshed on a pomegranate apple salad and short ribs—a hearty pairing to follow a whiskey tasting. A salted caramel pecan chocolate pecan pie left everyone with a sweet memory of a special evening together.

SALTED CARAMEL CHOCOLATE PECAN PIE

This is by far my favorite pie recipe. It is a combination of three perfect flavors—chocolate, pecans, and salted caramel—making one unforgettable dessert. Take the time to arrange the pecans on top into a perfect spiral for a showstopping presentation.

1¹/2 cups sugar

3/4 cup (1¹/2 sticks) butter, melted

1/3 cup all-purpose flour

1/3 cup 100 percent cacao unsweetened cocoa powder

1 tablespoon light corn syrup

1 teaspoon pure vanilla extract

3 large eggs

1 (9-inch) unbaked deep-dish piecrust

2 cups pecan halves

1/2 teaspoon sea salt

SALTED CARAMEL

3/4 cup sugar

1 tablespoon freshly squeezed lemon juice

1/4 cup water

1/3 cup heavy cream

1/4 cup (1/2 stick) butter

1/4 teaspoon salt

Makes 1 pie, approximately 10 servings

1. Preheat the oven to 350 degrees.
2. To make the chocolate filling, in a large bowl stir together the sugar, butter, flour, cocoa, corn syrup, and vanilla. Add the eggs, stirring until well blended. Pour the mixture into the piecrust. Bake for 35 minutes. The filling will be loose but will set as it cools. Remove the pie from the oven to cool on a wire rack.
3. Toast the pecan halves on a rimmed baking sheet in the heated oven until just fragrant, about 5 minutes (do not allow them to brown). Remove the baking sheet and allow the pecans to cool.
4. Meanwhile, prepare the caramel. Bring the sugar, lemon juice, and 1/4 cup of water to a boil in a medium saucepan over high heat. Do not stir. Boil, swirling occasionally after the sugar begins to change color, about 8 minutes, until dark amber. Do not walk away from the pan, as the sugar could burn quickly once it begins to change color. Remove the pan from the heat, then add the cream and butter. Stir the mixture constantly until the bubbling stops and the butter is incorporated, about 1 minute. Stir in the salt.
5. To assemble the pie, arrange the toasted pecan halves on the pie. Top with the warm caramel. Cool the pie for 10 minutes, then sprinkle with sea salt.

Note: You can also make this recipe into ten 3-inch mini pies. Adjust the baking time to 25 minutes.

MAKE IT AHEAD: This pie is very good served the day after it's made. Simply cover it and store it at room temperature.

GIFT GIVING

GIFT WRAPPING

Part of the fun of gifting around the holidays is the wrapping. The wrapping of a package is an extension of the gift, and I love to personalize the decoration for each recipient. Plus, thoughtfully trimmed packages look so beautiful under your Christmas tree in the weeks leading up to the big day. So start stocking up on different-sized boxes and get creative.

Here are some of my favorite ideas to make your gift wrapping extra special the whole year through:

- Craft paper is something you should always keep in your wrapping arsenal. It's a cheap, neutral base that can be dressed up easily.
- Join in the chalkboard trend by wrapping packages in simple black craft paper and using a white paint pen to personalize.
- Think beyond traditional wrapping paper. Instead, use a map of the place where the recipient is from or the newspaper's sports section for a sports fan.
- Don't confine yourself to wrapping all your gifts in paper. Tie a tea towel around a bottle of wine or use a vintage tablecloth to wrap a larger box, making the wrapping part of the present.
- Stick with a theme by wrapping a gift that corresponds with what's inside. If the gift is cooking related, for example, wrap it in paper that has butcher knife outlines. Add a bow and a wooden spoon, and the chef on your list will be thrilled.

MADE WITH LOVE

Homemade gifts are the best gifts. And when your holiday gift list includes not only family and friends but also coworkers, neighbors, teachers, and even the mail carrier, homemade treats make heartfelt, economical gifts that everyone appreciates.

I love making gifts that go beyond the present and foster family togetherness and traditions. I have a friend who makes cinnamon rolls as gifts for friends to bake on Christmas morning, and I love to give premade cookie dough so baking cookies for Santa can be fun and hassle-free. These buckeyes are a special treat, and the recipe makes a large amount, so they can be split up into several gifts.

PEANUT BUTTER CHOCOLATE-HAZELNUT BUCKEYES

1½ cups peanut butter

⅓ cup chocolate-hazelnut spread, such as Nutella

1 cup (2 sticks) butter, softened

½ teaspoon pure vanilla extract

6 cups powdered sugar

4 cups semisweet chocolate chips

Flaky sea salt

Makes approximately 30 buckeyes

1. In the bowl of an electric mixer fitted with the paddle attachment, mix together the peanut butter, chocolate-hazelnut spread, butter, vanilla, and powdered sugar. Using your hands, roll the mixture into 1-inch balls and place them on a baking sheet lined with parchment paper. Press a toothpick into the top of each ball (to be used later as the handle for dipping), and chill in the freezer until firm, at least 30 minutes.

2. Place the chocolate chips in a microwave-safe bowl and microwave for 30-second intervals, stirring after each until the chocolate is smooth. Hold the toothpick and dip the frozen balls into the melted chocolate. Leave a small portion of peanut butter showing at the top. Place the buckeyes back on the parchment paper, and sprinkle the tops with flaky sea salt. Once the chocolate has set, remove the toothpicks and refrigerate until serving.

COOKIES AND
COCKTAILS

The holidays can be crazy busy, and weekends book up fast with parties hosted by family and friends. I love hosting themed dessert parties where guests can drop by before or after other events.

For New Year's I hosted an early-evening "Cookies and Cocktails" hour, complete with confetti-filled balloons and glitter-covered champagne bottles. I made the party kid friendly so no babysitters were required and the entire family could join in.

Forget staying up until midnight. I popped the bubbly early to pour into a champagne tower, and everyone joined in to toast the new year.

GET THE LOOK

When deciding on decorations for this event, I was totally inspired by the amazing navy walls at the party's venue, City Farmhouse. I like combining weathered and worn pieces with modern clean lines, thus the sawhorse table juxtaposed with the modern glass serving pieces worked perfectly. I filled long rectangular glass floral containers with ice to display beautiful bottles of champagne. Cookies were showcased in glass jars filled with granulated sugar. Gold, white, and clear balloons filled with gold confetti were tied with navy satin ribbon.

A giant calligraphed banner with the party theme "Cheers, Y'all" was made to hang behind the main table, and temporary tattoos made for unexpected and amusing party favors.

THE MENU

Guests noshed on caviar served on French blini topped with crème fraîche and chives. Even the kids joined in the fun, gobbling up adorable penguin cookies with milk served in glass bottles with gold metal straws.

MAKE IT AHEAD

Bake or pick up sugar cookies the day before the party, and store them in an airtight container at room temperature overnight.

ENJOY THE PARTY!

When hosting a party that includes children, always have something for them to do. I love having a prepared craft that corresponds with the theme of the party for kids to work on while the adults socialize. Set up a play area away from the main food table that is totally kid-friendly so no one worries about them breaking anything.

At this party, kids made penguins out of black party cups and craft paper and used chalk to draw on black and navy paper. Fur throw pillows and penguin stuffed animals tucked in a teepee made for a soft and fun place to play.

HOW TO BUILD A CHAMPAGNE TOWER

The pouring of a champagne tower is a spectacular *Great Gatsby*–inspired party stunt that all your guests are sure to pull out their phones to video. Assemble the tower in advance during party setup, and pour the champagne once all the guests have arrived.

Start with a firm, solid base for your tower. A rimmed tray is a must to catch the overflow.

Always use coupe glasses (retro rounded saucer cups), not flutes. All the coupe glasses in the tower should be identical, and they are available at most party rental companies.

The tower is essentially made up of successively smaller square layers of glasses. For example, if the bottom layer is 10 glasses by 10 glasses, the layer above that would be 9 by 9, the layer above that 8 by 8, and so on.

Make sure each glass touches the surrounding glasses. When the tower is done right, you'll see diamond-shaped gaps between glasses. When building the next layer, center the stem of each glass over the diamond openings that were created by the layer below. Repeat this assembly process until there is a single coupe glass on top.

Once the tower is fully assembled, begin slowly pouring champagne from the top glass, and it will trickle downward, filling each glass.

KIDS' PARTIES

Children's birthday parties don't have to be filled with tacky store-bought decorations. Help your child pick a theme, and then think of ways to elevate the decor while still appealing to childhood sensibilities.

Emmaline has a January birthday, which is a little bit of a challenge because it always confines her party to indoor options. For her first birthday we threw a Winter ONEderland, complete with a biscuit bar, pink balloons, and owls (her favorite at the time) perched everywhere. The day before the party, it snowed 4 to 6 inches (which, in the South, is a lot). Having snow on the ground made the day even more magical as family was ushered in to warm up with hot apple cider and watch Emmaline open gifts by the fire.

For her second birthday, penguins took center stage for a Snowflake Brunch. I cut huge snowflakes out of white craft paper to create a mural on the wall behind the food table and hung dozens of smaller snowflakes from the ceiling. White and pink flowers were arranged in penguin-shaped vases, and penguin balloons wandered around the floor of the party (Emmaline's favorite part).

When children are young, parties include not only kids but also adults. Be mindful when planning food and drinks to have choices that will appeal to all ages. Provide small tables and seating for children, but also have comfortable accommodations for adults. You want everyone to have a good time and feel included.

WINTER MENU

The chill of winter flurries leaves us longing to curl up by the fire watching the falling snow through a frosted window, with a hearty meal roasting in the oven. Jack Frost stirs cravings of comfort food and childhood favorites that warm the soul.

The recipes in this chapter are almost exclusively family ones. Maybe it's the holidays that leave me sentimental about food memories, or it's the food memories that make the holidays special. Ask me my favorite Christmas gift I received as a child, and I literally can't name one (and it's not because the tree wasn't filled with packages every year). Ask me about my grandmother's pot roast or my mom's pound cake, and I can describe in detail the nuances of flavors, exactly how the smell wafted from the oven through the house, and the love that went into making it and sharing it with family.

There's no better season to stay inside and cook something exceptional with and for the ones you love. Gather around the table for a heartfelt meal that fills bellies and imprints joyful remembrance.

- Christmas Morning Breakfast
- Southern Skillet Cream Biscuits
- Chicken and Bacon Corn Chowder
- Chicken Pot Pie
- Lasagna
- Honey Mama's Pot Roast

- Chocolate Cake with Raspberry Buttercream
- White Chocolate Blondies
- Cream Cheese Pound Cake
- Chocolate Éclairs
- Peppermint Cheesecake

CHRISTMAS MORNING BREAKFAST

Christmas morning breakfast should be special and easy to put together—no one wants to be trapped in the kitchen cooking while everyone else is opening presents! I'm always sure to make something ahead of time that can be thrown in the oven so I don't miss one tear of wrapping paper.

SAUSAGE PINWHEELS

2 cups all-purpose flour

1/4 teaspoon baking soda

1 tablespoon baking powder

1 teaspoon salt

6 tablespoons unsalted butter, very cold

1 cup buttermilk

1/2 pound ground mild pork sausage

1/2 pound ground hot pork sausage

Makes 2 dozen pinwheels

> **MAKE IT AHEAD:** Place uncooked pinwheels in a freezer bag, separated by parchment paper, and freeze. Freeze for up to three months. When ready to bake, place the frozen pinwheels on an ungreased baking sheet, and bake at 350 degrees for 15 to 20 minutes.

1. Preheat the oven to 350 degrees.
2. Put the flour, baking soda, baking powder, and salt in the food processor. Pulse several times to mix. Cut the butter into small cubes before dropping into the food processor. Pulse until the mixture resembles coarse meal. Add the buttermilk and pulse until the dough just comes together. Dump onto a floured board, and knead for a minute or two. Using a rolling pin roll into a 14 x 10-inch rectangle about 1/4-inch thick.
3. In a large bowl mix the mild and hot sausage with your hands until just combined. Spread the sausage over rolled-out dough to within 1/2 inch of the edges. Roll the dough lengthwise to form a long roll. Using a serrated knife cut dough into 1/2-inch–thick slices.
4. Place the pinwheels on an ungreased baking sheet. Bake for 12 to 15 minutes until the sausage is cooked through. Drain off any juices. Serve warm or at room temperature.

SAUSAGE CHEESE BALLS

3 cups baking mix, such as Bisquick

1/2 pound ground mild pork sausage

1/2 pound ground hot pork sausage

4 cups grated Cheddar cheese

1/2 cup grated Parmesan cheese

3/4 cup milk

1 teaspoon fresh rosemary leaves, finely chopped

Makes 4 dozen balls

1. Preheat the oven to 350 degrees.
2. In a large bowl mix together baking mix, mild and hot sausage, Cheddar, Parmesan, milk, and rosemary with your hands or a spoon. Using an ice cream scoop, shape the mixture into 1-inch balls.
3. Place the sausage balls on an ungreased baking sheet. Bake for 18 to 20 minutes until the sausage is cooked through. Serve warm or at room temperature.

MAKE IT AHEAD: Place the uncooked balls on wax paper and put in a freezer bag. Freeze on a flat surface for up to three months. When ready to bake, place the frozen sausage balls on an ungreased baking sheet. Bake at 350 degrees for 20 to 25 minutes until the sausage is cooked through.

SOUTHERN SKILLET CREAM BISCUITS

As a Southern woman, I am required to be skilled in the making of a fluffy, flaky biscuit. When handling biscuit dough, work quickly, as you don't want the heat from your hands to melt the fat. Fold the dough over itself several times before rolling it out to make the flaky layers, and when cutting the biscuits, press straight down on the dough, being careful not to twist the biscuit cutter.

2 cups all-purpose flour

4 teaspoons baking powder

1/4 teaspoon baking soda

3/4 teaspoon salt

4 tablespoons cold butter, plus extra for preparing skillet

1 cup heavy cream, chilled

Makes 1 dozen (2-inch) biscuits

1. Preheat the oven to 450 degrees. Liberally butter a 9-inch cast-iron skillet.
2. In a large bowl combine the flour, baking powder, baking soda, and salt. Using your fingertips, pinch the butter into the flour mixture until the mixture looks like crumbs. (The faster, the better—you don't want the fat to melt.) Make a well in the center, and pour in the chilled cream. Stir just until the dough comes together. The dough will be very sticky.
3. Turn the dough onto a floured surface, dust the top with flour, and gently fold the dough over on itself 5 or 6 times. Using a rolling pin roll the dough into a 1-inch–thick round. Cut out biscuits with a 2-inch cutter, being sure to push straight down through the dough. Reform the scrap dough, working it as little as possible, and continue cutting. Place the biscuits in the buttered cast-iron skillet so that they just touch.
4. Bake until the biscuits are tall and light golden on top, about 15 to 20 minutes. Serve immediately.

MAKE IT AHEAD: Make the dough ahead of time, cut the biscuits, and place them in an airtight container. Refrigerate the biscuits for up to one day until ready to bake. Then place them in a buttered skillet and bake per the directions. You can also freeze the biscuits for up to one month. When you are ready to bake, place the frozen biscuits in a buttered skillet, and bake at 450 degrees for 20 to 25 minutes.

CHICKEN AND BACON CORN CHOWDER

This chicken chowder is a heaping bowl of goodness that pairs perfectly with just-out-of-the-oven, lightly browned Southern skillet cream biscuits (page 185). I tried to make this recipe lighter, and it just wasn't the same. Close your eyes, add the heavy cream, and enjoy a big bowl of happiness. Worry about your waistline come spring.

½ pound thick bacon, diced

5 stalks celery, diced

1 carrot, diced

2 medium Spanish onions, diced

3 garlic cloves, diced

2 medium russet potatoes, peeled and diced

8 ears fresh corn, kernels cut from the cob

2 to 3 teaspoons fresh thyme leaves

5 cups low-sodium chicken broth

¼ cup cornstarch

2½ cups heavy cream

1 rotisserie chicken, meat removed and shredded

Salt and freshly ground black pepper to taste

Makes 6 servings

1. Heat the bacon in a large pot over medium heat. Cook until the bacon fat is rendered and the meat is crisp, about 5 minutes. Add the celery, carrot, onions, and garlic. Reduce the heat to medium-low, and cook, stirring occasionally, until the vegetables begin to soften and the onion becomes translucent (not browned), about 10 minutes. Add the potatoes, corn, and thyme. Continue to cook, stirring occasionally, until the onions are fully soft, about 8 additional minutes.
2. Add the chicken broth to the pot. Bring the broth to a simmer over medium-high heat. Turn down the heat to medium, and simmer until the potatoes are tender, about 10 minutes.
3. In a separate bowl whisk the cornstarch into the heavy cream to prevent lumps. Add the cream and chicken to the soup pot. Return the chowder to a simmer, and season to taste with salt and pepper.

MAKE IT AHEAD: Make this soup before guests arrive, and leave it on the stove on simmer, stirring occasionally, to keep warm.

MAKE IT AHEAD: To make pot pies the day before, let filling cool completely, transfer to serving bowls, and top with the dough. Refrigerate until ready to bake per the directions.

CHICKEN POT PIE

Ina Garten is my favorite celebrity chef. Her recipes are tried and true and incredibly dependable. She seems lovable and approachable, and her cooking is elevated but still totally achievable. Just like Ina, my mom is a self-taught cook. As a child, my favorite thing she made was her chicken pot pie. I've combined Ina's and my mom's chicken pot pie recipes to create one perfect crowd-pleasing dish. What would I choose as my last meal on earth? This one.

PASTRY

3 cups all-purpose flour

1 teaspoon kosher salt

1 teaspoon baking powder

1/2 cup vegetable shortening

1/2 cup (1 stick) cold unsalted butter, diced

1/2 to 2/3 cup ice water

1 large egg beaten with 1 tablespoon water for egg wash

FILLING

5 cups chicken stock

2 chicken bouillon cubes

3/4 cup (11/2 sticks) unsalted butter

2 cups yellow onions, chopped (2 onions)

3/4 cup all-purpose flour

1/2 cup dry sherry

2 teaspoons kosher salt

1/2 teaspoon freshly ground black pepper

1/4 cup heavy cream

2 rotisserie chickens, meat removed and shredded

1 (16-ounce) package frozen peas and carrots

2 tablespoons minced fresh thyme

Makes 6 servings

1. Preheat the oven to 375 degrees.
2. To make the pastry, mix the flour, salt, and baking powder in the bowl of a food processor fitted with a metal blade. Add the shortening and butter, and pulse 10 times until the fat is the size of peas. With the motor running, add the ice water; process only enough to moisten the dough and have it just come together. Dump the dough onto a floured board, and knead it quickly into a disc. Wrap the dough in plastic, and allow it to rest in the refrigerator for at least 30 minutes.
3. To make the filling, in a small saucepan heat the chicken stock over medium-low heat, and dissolve the bouillon cubes in the stock. In a large pot or Dutch oven, melt the butter and sauté the onions over medium-low heat for 10 to 15 minutes until they are translucent. Add the flour and cook over low heat, stirring constantly, for 2 minutes. Add the hot chicken stock and sherry to the sauce. Simmer over low heat for 1 more minute, stirring, until thick. Add the salt, pepper, and heavy cream. Add the shredded chicken, peas and carrots, and thyme. Mix well.
4. Divide the filling equally among 6 (8-ounce) ovenproof bowls. Roll out the dough to 1/4-inch thickness, and cut 6 tops just larger than the serving bowls. Brush the outside edges of each bowl with the egg wash, then place the dough on top. Trim the circles to 1/2 inch larger than the top of the bowls. Crimp the dough to fold over the sides of each bowl, pressing to make them stick. Brush each with egg wash, and cut 4 slits in the top of each. Place on a baking sheet and bake for 1 hour until the tops are golden brown and the filling is bubbling hot.

Note: Sometimes I like to serve this family-style out of one large dish instead of individual bowls. Simply place the filling in a casserole dish, and cut the pastry one inch larger than the dish. Bake per the directions.

LASAGNA

There're aren't too many dishes more comforting than a huge helping of hot lasagna. Go ahead and make this lasagna, tuck it away in your freezer, and on the next cold night, treat your family to a warm, hearty dinner. They'll fight over the leftovers the next day, guaranteed.

1½ pounds ground beef

1 pound hot breakfast sausage

2 cloves garlic, minced

2 (14½-ounce) cans whole tomatoes

2 (6-ounce) cans tomato paste

4 tablespoons fresh parsley, finely chopped, divided

4 tablespoons fresh basil, finely chopped

2 teaspoons salt, divided

3 cups low-fat cottage cheese

2 large eggs, beaten

½ cup grated Parmesan cheese, plus more for garnish

1 (12-ounce) package oven-ready lasagna noodles

1 pound shredded mozzarella cheese, divided

Makes 12 servings

1. Preheat the oven to 350 degrees.
2. In a large skillet or saucepan combine the ground beef, sausage, and garlic. Cook over medium-high heat until the meat is browned. Drain the fat and return the meat to the pan. Add the tomatoes, tomato paste, 2 tablespoons of the parsley, basil, and 1 teaspoon of the salt. Let the sauce simmer for 30 to 45 minutes.
3. In a medium bowl mix the cottage cheese, beaten eggs, Parmesan, the remaining 2 tablespoons of parsley, and the remaining 1 teaspoon of salt. Stir until well combined.
4. To assemble the lasagna, spread 1 cup of the meat sauce in the bottom of a baking dish. Arrange 4 lasagna noodles on top of the sauce. Spoon half the cottage cheese mixture over the noodles, and spread evenly. Cover the cottage cheese with about a third of the mozzarella cheese. Spoon a little less than half the remaining meat sauce mixture over the top.
5. Repeat, ending with the meat sauce mixture. Sprinkle the top generously with extra Parmesan and the remaining mozzarella.
6. Bake for 20 to 30 minutes until the top is hot and bubbly.

MAKE IT AHEAD: Refrigerate the uncooked lasagna for up to two days. Bake per the directions, or freeze in an airtight container for up to six months. Bake the frozen lasagna at 350 degrees for 40 to 50 minutes, covering the top with foil if the cheese begins to brown.

HONEY MAMA'S POT ROAST

My grandmother's signature meal was pot roast. It was her go-to for feeding a large crowd, and she always made it in the same heavy aluminum Dutch oven. Now, whenever I make it, I'm reminded of her home, our Monday-night grandchildren dinners, and her love of entertaining.

Salt

Fresh cracked black pepper

1 (5-pound) chuck roast

3 tablespoons olive oil, plus additional if needed

2 onions, skin peeled and halved

6 to 8 carrots, cut into 2-inch pieces

1 cup red wine

2 to 3 cups beef stock

6 new potatoes, halved

3 sprigs fresh rosemary, or more to taste

3 sprigs fresh thyme, or more to taste

Makes 8 servings

1. Preheat the oven to 275 degrees.
2. Generously season the chuck roast with salt and pepper. Heat a large pot or Dutch oven over medium-high heat. Add the olive oil. When the oil in the pot is very hot (but not smoking), add the onions, browning them on one side and then on the other. Remove the onions to a plate. Brown the carrots the same way and remove them from the pot, adding them to the plate of onions.
3. If needed, add a bit more olive oil to the very hot pan. Place the meat in the pan, and sear all sides for about a minute on each side. Remove the roast to a plate. With the burner still on high, use red wine to deglaze the pan, scraping the bottom with a whisk to break up all the little brown bits.
4. When the bottom of the pan is sufficiently deglazed, place the roast back into the pan, and add enough beef stock to cover the meat halfway (about 3 cups). Add in the potatoes, onions, and carrots, as well as whole rosemary and thyme sprigs. Cover with the lid, and place in the preheated oven for about 4 hours until the meat is tender and the vegetables are soft.

MAKE IT AHEAD: This recipe is easily converted to a slow cooker. Follow the directions to sear the meat and vegetables in the slow cooker, and deglaze the insert. Cover and cook on low for 8 to 10 hours.

MAKE IT AHEAD: Make this cake the day before serving, and store it in the refrigerator. Wait to top it with raspberries until ready to serve (as they may bleed), and be sure to set it out with ample time before serving to let it come to room temperature.

CHOCOLATE CAKE WITH RASPBERRY BUTTERCREAM

This stunner makes the most beautiful birthday cake and Valentine's Day dessert. The chocolate cake is rich and decadent, perfectly stacked with sweet, fluffy raspberry buttercream and topped with fresh raspberries. I created it to celebrate my grandmother's Valentine's Day birthday and love to ice only in between the layers, leaving the outside bare to showcase the beautiful complementary colors and flavor profiles.

³/4 cup unsweetened cocoa powder, plus more to dust pan

2 cups all-purpose flour

2 cups sugar

2 teaspoons baking powder

1¹/2 teaspoons baking soda

1 teaspoon salt

1 teaspoon espresso powder

1 cup milk

¹/2 cup vegetable oil

2 large eggs

2 teaspoons pure vanilla extract

1 cup boiling water

RASPBERRY BUTTERCREAM ICING

1 cup (2 sticks) unsalted butter, softened

1 (8-ounce) package cream cheese, softened

7 cups powdered sugar, plus more for dusting, divided

6 tablespoons raspberry jam (pure fruit, no sugar added), divided

2 teaspoons pure vanilla extract

¹/2 teaspoon salt

2 tablespoons milk or cream

2 cups fresh raspberries for garnish

Makes 1 three-layer cake.
approximately 12 servings

1. Preheat the oven to 350 degrees. Butter three 8-inch round cake pans, dust with cocoa, then line each pan with parchment paper.
2. To make the cake, in the bowl of an electric mixer fitted with the paddle attachment, combine the flour, sugar, cocoa, baking powder, baking soda, salt, and espresso powder, and mix on low speed until well combined.
3. Add the milk, vegetable oil, eggs, and vanilla to the flour mixture, and mix on medium speed until well combined. Reduce the speed, and carefully add the boiling water to the cake batter. Beat on high speed for about 1 minute to add air to the batter.
4. Distribute the cake batter evenly among the three prepared cake pans. Bake for 25 to 30 minutes until a toothpick or cake tester inserted in the center comes out clean.
5. Remove the pans from the oven and allow the cakes to cool for about 10 minutes. Then remove the cakes from the pans, and cool completely before icing.
6. To make the icing, in the bowl of an electric mixer fitted with the whisk attachment, beat the butter until smooth. Add the cream cheese, and beat on a medium speed until it is fully combined and smooth. Add 1 cup of the powdered sugar, and mix on low speed until well combined. Add 1 tablespoon of the raspberry jam, the vanilla, and the salt, and mix on low speed until well combined.
7. In three parts, alternately add the remaining powdered sugar and raspberry jam, beginning and ending with the powdered sugar, beating well after each addition and finally beating until the icing is smooth and fluffy. Slowly add the 2 tablespoons of milk, and beat on high for another 20 seconds or so (this adds a shine to the icing).
8. To assemble the cake, use a serrated knife to level the tops of the cake layers, and place the first layer on a serving platter. Using an offset spatula, spread the top of that layer with ¹/2 inch of icing. Top with the trimmed layer, and repeat icing until all three layers are stacked.
9. Top the cake with raspberries and a dusting of powdered sugar.

WHITE CHOCOLATE BLONDIES

My mom would make me chocolate chip cookies without chocolate chips when I was a kid because I cidn't like chocolate. I'm still not a big "chocolate person." *Gasp*—I know! These blondies are basically brownies made with white chocolate instead of traditional semisweet chocolate. They're buttery, chewy, speckled with pecans, and they can win over any chocoholic.

3/4 cup (5 ounces) white chocolate chips

1/2 cup (1 stick) unsalted butter

3/4 cup sugar

2 large eggs, room temperature

1 1/2 teaspoons pure vanilla extract

1/8 teaspoon salt

1 1/2 cups all-purpose flour

1 cup pecans, chopped

Makes 16 bars

1. Preheat the oven to 325 degrees. Line a 9 x 9-inch pan with parchment paper.
2. Place the white chocolate and butter in a microwave-safe bowl. Microwave on high for 30-second intervals, stirring after each until the mixture is melted and smooth (it's okay if the chocolate and butter mixture seems separated). Allow to cool 1 to 2 minutes.
3. Add the sugar, and using a rubber spatula, stir until well incorporated. Stir in the eggs and vanilla until combined. Add the salt, flour, and pecans, and stir until well incorporated and the nuts are evenly dispersed.
4. Pour the batter into the prepared baking pan, and bake for 35 to 40 minutes until golden brown and the center is still soft. Let the blondies cool completely before slicing them into 2-inch squares. These treats are best served at room temperature.

MAKE IT AHEAD: Make the blondies a day in advance, and store them in an airtight container at room temperature.

CREAM CHEESE POUND CAKE

This is my go-to, perfect-for-any-occasion dessert that has been a longtime headliner in my family's recipe box. I have made it for birthdays, brunches, hostess gifts, and Christmas presents. It has a wonderfully rich and buttery flavor and a moist texture, and it stores (or even freezes) beautifully.

1½ cups (3 sticks) butter, softened

1 (8-ounce) package cream cheese, softened

3 cups sugar

6 large eggs, room temperature

1 teaspoon salt

¼ cup buttermilk

2 teaspoons pure vanilla extract

1 teaspoon almond extract

3 cups all-purpose flour

Makes 12 servings

1. Preheat the oven to 325 degrees. Butter and flour a 10-inch tube pan (or two snowflake pans).
2. In an electric mixture fitted with the paddle attachment, cream the butter and cream cheese on medium speed until smooth. Add the sugar gradually, beating until the mixture is fluffy. Add the eggs, one at a time, beating the batter well after each addition. Add the salt, buttermilk, vanilla, and almond extract, and blend the batter until smooth. Add the flour, and mix until it is just incorporated.
3. Pour the batter into the prepared pan. Bake for 1 hour and 20 minutes until a wooden pick inserted into the center of the cake comes out clean. Cool the cake in the pan for 10 minutes, and then invert it onto a serving plate.

Note: To create the snowflake shape, I used a Nordic Ware snowflake pan, but you can also use a tube pan.

MAKE IT AHEAD: Make this cake up to three days in advance and store it at room temperature, or freeze it in an airtight container for up to three months.

CHOCOLATE ÉCLAIRS

During college my brother and I ventured to Europe for a whirlwind trip across the continent—an adventure outside both of our comfort zones. In Paris, I remember standing at the counter of a pastry shop with dozens of Frenchmen quickly moving through as they ordered coffee and croissants. When the server finally looked to me, the extent of my French was revealed as I muttered, "Éclair, s'il vous plaît" and pointed in the direction of the pastries. I quickly found out that was all the French I really needed to know. I came home with one plan: to learn how to make chocolate éclairs . . . and maybe learn a little more French.

PASTRY

1 cup boiling water

1/2 cup (1 stick) unsalted butter

1 cup all-purpose flour

1/4 teaspoon salt

4 large eggs

CUSTARD FILLING

1/2 cup sugar

2 tablespoons cornstarch

1/2 teaspoon salt

1 cup milk

1 cup half-and-half

2 large eggs

1 teaspoon pure vanilla extract

CHOCOLATE ICING

3 ounces unsweetened chocolate

1/4 cup water

2 tablespoons butter

1/4 teaspoon salt

2 cups powdered sugar, sifted

1/2 teaspoon pure vanilla extract

Makes 12 éclairs

1. To make the pastry, preheat the oven to 450 degrees. Line two baking sheets with baking mats or parchment paper.
2. In a medium saucepan add the butter to the boiling water. Cook over medium heat until the butter is melted, stirring constantly. All at once, add the flour and salt. Cook for 1 minute, stirring constantly with a wooden spoon, until the mixture becomes smooth and forms a soft ball. Remove the pan from the heat. Add the eggs one at a time, beating vigorously after each addition. Beat until the dough is smooth.
3. Transfer the mixture to a pastry bag, and cut 1 inch off the tip. Pipe 1 x 3-inch oblong shapes. Bake for 15 minutes. Reduce the oven temperature to 325 degrees. Bake for 20 to 25 minutes longer. Cool the pan on a wire rack.
4. To make the custard filling, mix the sugar, cornstarch, and salt in a saucepan. Whisk in the milk, half-and-half, and eggs. Bring the mixture to a boil over medium heat, stirring constantly with a wooden spoon. Remove the pan from the heat. Stir in the vanilla. Cool completely (put the bowl in an ice bath to speed up cooling).
5. Split each éclair lengthwise with a serrated knife. Fill with the custard.
6. To make the chocolate icing, in a saucepan combine the chocolate, water, butter, and salt. Cook over medium heat until the chocolate and butter are melted. Remove from the heat. Whisk in the powdered sugar and vanilla until smooth. Spread the icing over the éclairs.
7. Chill the éclairs uncovered for at least 1 hour to set the icing. Served chilled.

MAKE IT AHEAD: Make the éclairs a day before, and store them in the refrigerator in an airtight container.

PEPPERMINT CHEESECAKE

This frozen peppermint cheesecake is the quintessential Christmas confection. It has a wonderfully festive appearance, a cool holiday peppermint filling, and a decadent chocolate crust—and it can be prepared well in advance. It is the perfect sweet ending to any holiday celebration.

CRUST

1½ cups chocolate sandwich cookie crumbs (pulsed in the bowl of a food processor)

¼ cup sugar

¼ cup (½ stick) butter, melted

FILLING

1 (8-ounce) package cream cheese, softened

1 (14-ounce) can sweetened condensed milk

1 cup crushed hard peppermint candy

3 drops of red food coloring

2 cups heavy cream, whipped

Whipped cream for garnish

Whole and crushed hard peppermint for garnish

Hot chocolate sauce for garnish

Makes 1 cheesecake.
approximately 12 servings

1. To make the crust, combine the chocolate cookie crumbs, sugar, and butter in a bowl, and mix well until it resembles wet sand. Press in the bottom and up the sides of a 9-inch springform pan. Freeze until set, about 30 minutes.

2. To make the filling, in the bowl of an electric mixer fitted with the whisk attachment, beat the cream cheese on high speed until fluffy. Add the sweetened condensed milk, crushed peppermint candy, and food coloring (one drop at a time, mixing after each until you achieve the desired color), and mix well. Remove the bowl from the mixer. Using a rubber spatula, fold in the 2 cups of whipped heavy cream until just combined. Pour the filling into the chilled crust. Freeze, covered, until set, at least 24 hours.

3. Before serving, allow the cheesecake to sit at room temperature about 10 minutes to make it easier to slice. Unlatch the springform pan and slice. Drizzle each slice with hot chocolate sauce, and garnish with whipped cream and peppermint candy.

MAKE IT AHEAD: Make this cheesecake up to three months in advance, and store it in an airtight container in the freezer.

MENUS

Intimate dinner parties are one of my favorite ways to gather the ones we love. Use this seasonal menu guide to orchestrate your next flawless occasion.

Spring

Spiked Pomegranate Mint Lemonade, page 32

Turkey Burgers, page 36

Grilled Avocados with Pico de Gallo, page 35

Deviled Eggs with Bacon Jam, page 40

Lemon Blueberry Tart, page 43

Summer

The Ultimate Skinny Margarita, page 31

Peach Caprese Salad, page 81

Fish Tacos with Grilled Corn Slaw and Strawberry Mango Salsa, page 84–85

Blackberry Cobbler with Homemade Vanilla Ice Cream, page 86

Fall

Charcuterie Platter, page 134

Skillet Cheddar Dill Cornbread, page 141

Smoked Brisket Chili, page 142

Chocolate-Hazelnut Brownies with Pretzel Graham Cracker Crust, page 153

Winter

Popovers, page 137

Chicken Pot Pie, page 189

Chocolate Cake with Raspberry Buttercream, page 195

ACKNOWLEDGMENTS

A huge thank you to my family for their constant love and support. To my husband, Brent, for being my harshest critic, my number one taste-tester, and my greatest love. To my daughter Emmaline for stealing the show at every photoshoot and being my greatest joy. And to my sweet baby girl, who will be born around the release of this book—we can't wait for you to join the party!

Mom, thank you for schlepping props, food, flowers, and everything in between. I couldn't have done the project without you. To Claire, for taking such good care of E while I was working.

To Amy Cherry, my master photographer and friend, who always knew exactly what I wanted before I ever had to say anything. Working with you on this project was such fun! To Abi McGinnis, whose beautiful calligraphy graced almost every shoot—I can never thank you enough for your friendship and support.

Elizabeth Mayhew, thank you for your unbelievable support, guidance, and encouragement throughout this project. It wouldn't have happened without you! To Molly Hodgin for giving this project a shot. To Mary Hooper for "getting me" in the very important design of this book. And to my editor Dawn Hollomon for helping create the book I've always dreamed of.

Thank you to all the local Nashville business owners who loaned me props, locations, food, your time and expertise: it was an honor to work with you, and I hope I have showcased your talents to the level that they deserve. To my friends and family who let me shoot at their homes, borrow their dishes, and use their children as models, I'm so thrilled to have you included in such a dream project.

Finally, to all my StylingMyEveryday.com followers: you are the reason I created this. Your encouragement and constant support mean so much!

SOURCES AND CREDITS

FAIRY-TALE FERN WHITE LINEN LUNCHEON, PAGES 2–5

Casafina Forum White Salad/Dessert Plate plates, Juliska and Simon Pearce glass pitchers glass pitchers, Simon Pearce bowls, Orrefors Regina crystal candlesticks, Simon Pearce Woodbury wine glassware: The Registry (theregistryfranklin.com); hurricanes, Montes Doggett fruit bowls, carafe: Digs Interiors (digsinteriors.com); Astier de Villatte platter, Pom Pom at Home Olivier linen tablecloth and napkins: The Iron Gate (theirongateonline.net); Mirage Vessel votives: Anthropologie (anthropologie.com); olive wood paddle boards: West Elm (westelm.com); vanilla bean macarons, The Painted Cupcake (thepaintedcupcake.com); handcrafted wooden bench: The Barn Door Co.; fashion: Emmaline (emmalineboutique.com); calligraphy by Abi McGinnis of Abigail T. Calligraphy (abigailtcalligraphy.com)

BREAKFAST IN BED, PAGE 8

Breakfast tray: Williams-Sonoma (williams-sonoma.com); charm bracelet: Altruette (altruette.com)

EASTER EGG HUNT, PAGES 10–13

Location: Homestead Manor (homesteadmanor.com); children's clothing, Easter baskets, Blabla bunnies: Magpies (magpiesnashville.com); flowers: Garden Delights (gardendelights.net); macarons: Sweet Darling Pâtisserie (sweetdarlingpatisserie.com); calligraphy by Abi McGinnis of Abigail T. Calligraphy (abigailtcalligraphy.com); fashion: Draper James (draperjames.com)

Models: Cece and Charlotte McClellan, Harper and Brantley Davis, Maggie Tucker of Magpies, Sara Darling of Sweet Darling Pâtisserie

MOTHER'S DAY TEA PARTY, PAGES 18–21

Food: Puffy Muffin (puffymuffin.com); monogrammed handkerchiefs: Sew What Gifts (sewwhatgifts.com); calligraphy by Abi McGinnis of Abigail T. Calligraphy (abigailtcalligraphy.com)

Models: Kathleen Horrell, Peggy Franks, Emmaline Jacobs

FOURTH OF JULY POOL PARTY, PAGES 50–53

Children's clothing: The Beaufort Bonnet Company (thebeaufortbonnetcompany.com); gelato: Legato Gelato (legatogelato.com); blue enamel plates: Pottery Barn (potterybarn.com); sparklers: Sparklers Online (sparklersonline.com); Fashion: Draper James (draperjames.com)

Model: Terri-Ann Nicholl of Legato Gelato

BACKYARD MOVIE NIGHT, PAGES 56–59

Fashion, pillows, napkins: Draper James (draperjames.com)

Models: Elizabeth, Annie, and Graham Walker

HOSTESS BASKETS, PAGES 62–63

Corkcicle Canteen: Sew What Gifts (sewwhatgifts.com); lantern: Target (target.com); Weck carafe: Tin Cottage (tincottage.com); Bongo Java coffee, Blackberry Patch syrup, pancake mix: White's Mercantile (whitesmercantile.com); calligraphy by Abi McGinnis of Abigail T. Calligraphy (abigailtcalligraphy.com)

MILKSHAKE SOCIAL, PAGES 64–67

Plates and glasses: CB2 (cb2.com); gold straws: W&P Design (wandpdesign.com); cotton candy milkshake glasses: Target (target.com); flamingo: Pottery Barn Kids (potterybarnkids.com); backdrop: Kate Spade (katespade.com); vintage milkshake machine: The Barn Door Co.

AUTUMN TAILGATE, PAGES 98–102

Vintage props: Scarlett Scales (scarlettscales.com) and Tin Cottage (tincottage.com); vintage truck: Ray Clark; fashion: Draper James (draperjames.com); calligraphy by Abi McGinnis of Abigail T. Calligraphy (abigailtcalligraphy.com)

Model: Sarah Basel

WINE-TASTING PARTY, PAGE 106

Catering: MStreet Catering & Events (MStreetNashville.com); wine: The Bottle Shop (bottleshop-mcewen.com); serving pieces, Vietri plates, Mud Pie salt dishes, Fog Linen napkins: Two Old Hippies (twooldhippies.com); charcuterie board: Tin Cottage (tincottage.com); paper runners, banner tags, pencils, wine scorecards and KnobStoppers: Hester & Cook (hesterandcook.com)

Models: Lauren and Wade Weaver, Cherilyn and Ray Clark, Katie and Brent Jacobs

PIE PARTY, PAGES 108–111

Charcuterie board, bottle opener, Match Italian pewter wine carafe, Ben Caldwell vine handle copper servers, Match Luisa rectangular platter: AshBlue (ashblue.com); brass fox wine accessory set, fox serving tray, and log holder: Target (target.com); mercury hurricane: West Elm (westelm.com); ruffled pie dish: Williams-Sonoma (williams-sonoma.com)

HARVEST PICNIC, PAGES 118–121

Location: Bloomsbury Farm (bloomsburyfarms.com), burlap lunch totes: Tin Cottage (tincottage.com); acorn lunch tags: Hester & Cook (hesterandcook.com); fashion: Draper James (draperjames.com)

Model: Lauren Palmer of Bloomsbury Farm (bloomsburyfarms.com)

S'MORES BAR, PAGE 127

Weck jars and berry holders: Tin Cottage (tincottage.com)

GINGERBREAD HOUSE DECORATING PARTY, PAGES 158–161

Location: The Red House (ourredhouse.com); table, chairs, bench, and glass hurricanes: The Barn Door Co.; cookies: Baked by Ash (bakedbyash.com); fashion: Draper James (draperjames.com); paper table coverings: Hester & Cook for Draper James (hesterandcook.com)

Models: Annie and Graham Walker, Lily Wadlington, Holt Adcock, Camden Blanch, Whitt McGinnis, Emmaline Jacobs

HOT CHOCOLATE PARTY, PAGES 164–165

Location: The Red House (ourredhouse.com); Juliska ramekins, ice bucket, serving tray, glasses, and ghost double wall glass carafe: COLOR (colorathome.com); William Yeoward Country cake stand, LeJacquard Tivoli napkins in poppy, Juliska Country Estate mugs, and Juliska Victor decanter: The Registry (theregistryfranklin.com)

WHISKEY TASTING, PAGES 166–167

Location: Homestead Manor (homesteadmanor.com); invitation suite: Currier Stevens and Bonnie Cross of Tenn Hens Design (tennhens.com); calligraphy by Val Cole; moss table runner, whiskey rocks, and whiskey decanter: Tin Cottage (tincottage.com); antlers and lighting: The Barn Door Co.

Model: Brooke Webb of KBStyled (kbstyled.com)

COOKIES AND COCKTAILS, PAGES 174–177

Location: City Farmhouse (cityfarmhousefranklin.com); temporary tattoos: Love & Lion (loveandlion.com); sparkling wine: Le Grand Courtâge (legrandcourtage.com); cookies: Triple Crown Bakery (triplecrownbakery.com); balloons: Oh Shiny Paper Co. (ohshinypaper.co); calligraphy by Abi McGinnis of Abigail T. Calligraphy (abigailtcalligraphy.com)

Models: Leah Hasson of Love & Lion (loveandlion.com), Bennett Brown, Emmaline Jacobs

PHOTO CREDITS

RECIPE INDEX

ABOUT THE AUTHOR

KATIE JACOBS is a stylist, photographer, graphic designer, and foodie. A fourth-generation Nashvillian, she's been featured in *Martha Stewart Living*, *Southern Living*, *Southern Living Weddings*, and *Nashville Lifestyles* as well as on *Inspired By This*, *Fashionable Hostess*, and *The Scout Guide*. She has contributed content for Reese Witherspoon's lifestyle brand Draper James, Pottery Barn, and Le Grand Courtâge, among others. Learn more on Katie's food and lifestyle blog, StylingMyEveryday.com.